DARIO FO

KT-375-297

Accidental Death of an Anarchist

translated by
SIMON NYE

with commentary and notes by
JOSEPH FARRELL, *Professor of Italian, University of Strathclyde*

methuen | drama

LONDON · NEW YORK · OXFORD · NEW DELHI · SYDNEY

METHUEN DRAMA
Bloomsbury Publishing Plc
50 Bedford Square, London, WC1B 3DP, UK
1385 Broadway, New York, NY 10018, USA

BLOOMSBURY, METHUEN DRAMA and the Methuen Drama logo
are trademarks of Bloomsbury Publishing Plc

This edition first published in the United Kingdom in 2003
by Methuen Publishing Ltd
Reissued with additional material and a new cover design 2005;
reissued with a new cover design 2009
This translation of *Accidental Death of an Anarchist*
first published in the United Kingdom
in 2003 by Methuen Drama

Reprinted 2007, 2008, 2009, 2010, 2011, 2012 (twice), 2013,
2014, 2015, 2016 (three times), 2017 (twice), 2018, 2020

Note to the Reader
This is a playscript and should be read as such.

A catalogue record for this book is available from the British Library.

A catalog record for this book is available from the Library of Congress.

ISBN: PB: 978-0-4137-7267-1

Series: Student Editions

Typeset by SX Composing DTP, Rayleigh, Essex
Printed and bound in Great Britain

To find out more about our authors and books visit
www.bloomsbury.com and sign up for our newsletters.

Contents

Dario Fo

1926 Dario Fo is born in the village of San Giano in
Lombardy, northern Italy. His father, Felice, is a
station-master, his mother, Pina Rota, a woman of
peasant stock. Dario is the oldest of three, with one
brother, Fulvio, and one sister, Bianca.

1936 Felice Fo is moved by the railway authorities to Porto
Valtraglia, on the shores of Lake Maggiore, where
Dario spends the rest of his childhood. In his Nobel
prize-winning speech in Stockholm, he continued to
underline his debt to the *fabulatori,* story-tellers, of the
village. These were not professional performers but
fishermen or glassblowers who, while repairing nets or
blowing molten glass, recounted fantastic tales, a blend
of references to local people and episodes of pure
fantasy.

1940 Italy joins the war on the side of Nazi Germany. Dario
begins commuting daily to Milan, to study at the
Brera, a complex of institutes which included a high
school, an art college and the famous art gallery.

1943 The Allies land in Sicily. Mussolini is overthrown in
Rome, imprisoned then released by German forces.

1944 Mussolini chooses Salò, on Lake Garda, as capital of
his new Republic. Northern Italy, including Dario's
home village, comes under its control. Dario is called
up by the Republic of Salò. He joins the army, then
deserts, and although not taking an active part in the
Resistance, spends months in hiding.

1945 Resumes commuting daily to Milan, where he studies
art at the Brera and enrols to study architecture at the
Politecnico. Dario is caught up in the stimulating
intellectual life of post-Liberation Milan, reading
authors and seeing the work of artists who had been
banned under Fascism. His aim is to be a painter, and

he puts on his first art exhibition in the city of Bergamo.

1947 During the daily journeys to Milan, Dario starts entertaining commuters with sketches and songs of his own. He lives a Bohemian life in Milan, meeting artists and writers, and taking part with friends in 'raids' on theatres, where they buy seats on purpose to boo and jeer well-established writers and actors, especially those who have been compromised by Fascism.

1948 First venture into theatre, with a now lost piece, *The Tresa Divides Us,* performed by him and his friends, satirising the division of Italy between Communists and Christian Democrats.

1949 Mother, brother and sister move to Milan. Dario has a nervous breakdown and abandons his study of architecture. He continues painting all his life.

1950 Dario meets the actor Franco Parenti, who encourages him to continue writing and performing *Poer nano* (*Poor Sod*), a series of monologues. These tales overturn traditional heroes and villains, telling, for instance, the story of David and Goliath from the perspective of a good-hearted, overgrown chump, called Goliath.

1951 While playing in a review called *Seven Days in Milan,* he meets Franca Rame, performing in the same show. Franca belongs to a family company of travelling players who can trace their theatrical pedigree back to the eighteenth century.

1952 Appears in a variety show, *Cocoricò,* in a cast which includes Giustino Durano.

1953 Records his first song, 'The Moon is a Lightbulb'. Writes many songs, mainly whimsical or satirical, some for other singers. Music is an intrinsic part of his theatre at all phases of his career.

1953 Establishes, with Franco Parenti and Giustino Durano, his first theatre company, The Uprights. The three stage at the Piccolo Teatro in Milan a satirical cabaret entitled *A Poke in the Eye.* Franca Rame is one of the performers.

1954   Franca and Dario marry. Their lives as performers, writers and political activists are from that point inseparable. *Madhouse for the Sane,* the second cabaret review for the same company.

1955   In spite of the success of the second show, the company splits up and the members go their own way. Dario and Franca's only son, Jacopo, is born. The family move to Rome, where Dario intends to try his luck in cinema, both as scriptwriter and actor.

1956   Writes and stars in a film, *Lo Svitato (Screwball),* directed by Carlo Lizzani, with Franca as female lead. The film is not a great success.

1958   The couple return to Milan and to theatre. They set up the Compagnia Fo-Rame, with Dario as writer, actor, director, stage-designer. *Thieves, Mannequins and Nude Women,* a programme of four one-act farces all by Dario is a success with critics and public. Second set of one-act farces, *Comica finale*, is staged in Turin.

1959   The staging of *Archangels Don't Play Pinball* at the Odeon in Milan marks the beginning of what is later tagged Fo's 'bourgeois period'. Fo and Rame make their name in the established theatres of the great cities of Italy. The years of Italy's 'economic miracle'.

1960   Premiere of *He Had Two Pistols and Black and White Eyes*, a comedy satirising corruption in the building trade. First foreign production of his work: *Archangels Don't Play Pinball* performed in Zagreb.

1961   *He Who Steals a Foot Is Lucky in Love*, a modern version of the myth of Daphne and Apollo, with satirical overtones. *Thieves, Mannequins and Nude Women* is performed in Stockholm.

1962   Dario and Franca are invited, on a trial basis, to present a small programme *Who's Seen It?* on a new TV channel, RAI2. Their ratings lead to their being asked to present on the main channel *Canzonissima* (The Big Song), RAI's main Saturday evening variety spectacular. Whimsical sketches are expected, but Dario's pieces are hard-hitting, comic satires on issues of the day. Ratings soar, but questions are asked in

parliament and the couple receive death threats.
During a building workers' strike, Dario is refused
permission to broadcast a sketch on accidents at work,
but will not make changes. The couple walk out. The
story makes headlines, guaranteeing the couple's
celebrity.

1963   Return to the Odeon, Milan, with *Isabella, Three
Caravels and a Con-man,* a comedy on Christopher
Columbus at the Spanish court, which also reflects
Dario's experience in the offices of RAI.

1964   *Seventh: Steal a Little Less* goes on tour to some fifty-
one venues. Over 200,000 spectators see the show.

1965   *Always Blame the Devil,* Dario's first work set in the
Middle Ages.

1966   *I Think It Over and Sing About It,* a programme of
traditional peasant and workers' songs. Fo's
knowledge of the world of popular culture deepens.

1967   Adaptation of a play by the French writer, Georges
Michel, *The Sunday Stroll.* Also writes *Toss the Lady
Out,* set in a mock-up of a circus, a bitter attack on the
American involvement in Vietnam.

1968   Fundamental change of course. Break with 'bourgeois
theatre' to forge a new style of popular theatre. 'We
were tired of being the jesters of the bourgeoisie, on
whom our criticisms had now the effect of an alka-
seltzer, so we decided to become the jesters of the
proletariat.' Disbands own company to establish a
theatrical co-operative, Nuova Scena. Gives up writing
comedy, and returns to farce. His plays become
explicitly political in intention. Abandons the great
theatres in the big cities to play to working-class
people in an 'alternative circuit' of venues managed by
ARCI, the cultural and recreational organisation
associated with the Communist party. *Grand
Pantomime with Puppets Small, Medium and Large,* in
which he ridicules the church, the army and big
business. During the year, the company gives some 370
performances in around 125 centres, one of which is a
steelworks in Brescia occupied by striking workers. For

this, Dario and Franca receive a summons from the local magistrate, the first of many.

1969 *I Think It Over and Sing About It, No 2*, directed by Fo with traditional and freshly written material. Performance in New York of two of the one-act farces, first productions in English. For operational purposes, the Nuova Scena co-operative divides into three troupes, one headed by the playwright, Vittorio Franceschi, the second by Franca Rame and the third consisting of Dario alone. Franca, with others, performs two one-act plays written by Fo: *The Worker Knows 300 Words, the Boss 1000; That's Why He Is the Boss,* and *The Boss's Funeral.* Dario stages *Mistero Buffo,* a series of sketches from medieval sources, sometimes very substantially rewritten, all performed by him alone on stage. Dario models himself on the *giullare* (jester), an entertainer from medieval theatre.

1970 Growing gulf with Communist party leads to the break-up of Nuova Scena. Dario and Franca found La Comune, which retains club membership and the co-operative structure. The new company finds a base in Il Capannone, a warehouse in a working-class area of Milan. *I'd Rather Die Tonight If I Thought It Had All Been In Vain,* a programme of songs and readings on the Italian and Palestinian Resistance staged in the new venue. First performances of *Accidental Death of an Anarchist.*

1971 *All Together! All United! Excuse Me, Isn't That the Boss?* a new play, subtitled *Workers' Struggles 1911–22.*

1972 Several new works: *Fedayeen,* a series of readings by Palestinian exiles and militants, *Accidental Death of an Anarchist and Other Subversives,* an updated version dealing with the mysterious death of the publisher, Giangiacomo Feltrinelli, *Order by GOOOOOOOOD!* and *Knock! Knock! Who's There?,* on the deaths of Pinelli and Feltrinelli. Franca Rame sets up Red Aid, a support group for imprisoned left-wing militants and their families. The terrorist campaign at its height. Dario and Franca opposed to the use of terror as a political strategy, but are now the focus of police attention, their phone tapped, they themselves shadowed by police officers. Frequent court appearances.

1973   Kidnap and rape of Franca by right-wing terrorists acting, as proved later by the report by Judge Guido Salvini, with the connivance of the *carabinieri*, Italy's main police force. Dario arrested in Sardinia for allegedly failing to comply with a demand from the police to enter the theatre where he was rehearsing. La Comune, riven by internal disputes, breaks up. New company, The Theatrical Collective 'La Comune' Directed by Dario Fo established. First work *The People's War in Chile*, a series of monologues and one-act pieces written in protest over the coup d'état in Chile which ousted the Marxist President, Salvador Allende.

1974   The new company takes over the Palazzina Liberty, a disused art nouveau building in Milan. Originally the City Council agreed to the lease, but reneged on the deal. The building is occupied, court cases drag on for years. *Can't Pay? Won't Pay!* premiered in the new venue.

1975   Dario nominated, unsuccessfully, for Nobel Prize. Premiere of *The Kidnap of Fanfani*, a political fantasy on the imaginary kidnap of Christian Democrat leader, Amintore Fanfani. Dario and Franca, with various members of the company, visit China.

1976   *Mum's Marijuana Is Best*, an attack on the use of drugs, written at the request of parents of the locality of Palazzina Liberty.

1977   Return to TV for first time since 1962. Several plays to be broadcast from the Palazzina, with Dario in full control as director, designer, writer and performer. Works shown include *Can't Pay? Won't Pay!*, a rewritten version of *Seventh: Steal a Little Less*, and *Mistero Buffo*. The screening of this last work unleashes a storm of protest, with long articles in the press, debates in Parliament, complaints to the magistrates and a denunciation from the Vatican that the play is 'disgusting, crass and degrading [. . .] a work of blasphemy'. The final programme is a series of not very successful but wholly new pieces entitled *Let's Talk About Women,* the first in a series of feminist works by Franca and Dario, which marks a new phase in Dario's output. *All Bed, Board and Church,* a substantially rewritten and rethought series of feminist monologues, is staged in Milan.

1978   *The Tale of a Tiger,* a one-man monologue based on a story Fo had heard in China. *We Can't Pay? We Won't Pay!,* a translation by Lino Pertile, adapted by Rob Walker, becomes the first Fo play to be staged in Britain. Writes a tragedy, never performed, based on the kidnapping and murder that year of the Christian Democrat leader, Aldo Moro. Finally evicted from Palazzina Liberty, the last theatre of his own. Invited by La Scala to produce a touring production of Stravinsky's *The Soldier's Tale.*

1979   Fo wins damages over a claim that during the last phase of the war he had been involved in the slaughter of Resistance fighters.

1980   Dario and Franca refused entry to the USA, allegedly on the grounds of their involvement with Red Aid. Their American hosts organise in New York *An Evening Without Dario Fo and Franca Rame,* which attracts the support of Martin Scorsese, Arthur Miller, Joe Chaikin and Norman Mailer. *Accidental Death of an Anarchist* opens in London's West End.

1981   *Trumpets and Raspberries* written in ten days and staged in Milan. *The Opera of Guffaws,* a work initially commissioned by the Berliner Ensemble as a new production of Bertolt Brecht's *Threepenny Opera* but then rejected, opens in Turin.

1982   *Obscene Fables,* three one-man pieces based on medieval Provençal sources. Dario and Franca make first visit to Britain to perform at the Riverside Studios, London. *Female Parts,* translations of the recent

feminist monologues, performed at the National
Theatre, London.

1983   Dario and Franca again refused permission to visit the
USA. *The Open Couple*, a comedy with
autobiographical overtones, premieres in Stockholm.

1984   Exhibition of Fo's paintings tours Italy. Visit to Buenos
Aires, where they are a target of protests, culminating
in the throwing of a tear-gas bomb inside the theatre.
Dario and Franca perform at the Edinburgh Festival.
Accidental Death of an Anarchist opens in New York.
Dario and Franca granted visa to perform in the USA.
Almost by Chance a Woman: Elizabeth, a play
featuring Elizabeth I of England, and making reference
to Shakespeare, opens with Franca in the title role and
Dario taking a cross-dressing part as the Queen's
maid.

1985   *Hellequin, Harlekin, Arlecchino*, a re-examination of
the Harlequin character, staged at the Venice Biennale.

1986   Performance tour of the USA. Franca returns to the
Edinburgh Festival, where she is joined by Dario, who
does not perform. A visit to the Traverse Theatre to
see Tilda Swinton in *Man to Man* provides the
inspiration for *An Ordinary Day*. *Kidnapping
Francesca* opens in Trieste.

1987   *An Ordinary Day* opens in a double bill with *Open
Couple*, Dario directing, Franca performing. Dario
directs Rossini's opera *The Barber of Seville* in
Amsterdam. Franca stuns Italy by announcing on a
television show that she and Dario are separating. The
two reconciled after a couple of months. Returns to
the USA to direct *Archangels Don't Play Pinball* in
Cambridge, Massachusetts. Publishes *Tricks of the
Trade*, a compilation of talks, workshops and articles
in which he expounds his views of theatre and
stagecraft.

1988   *Forced Transmission*, an eight-part series on television.

1989   *The Pope and the Witch*, on drugs and birth-control.
Tour to Brazil.

1990   Directs two short plays by Molière at the Comédie

Française in Paris. *Shhhhh . . . We're Falling!*, a play on Aids.

1991 *Johan Padan Discovers the Americas*, a dramatic-satirical monologue written in response to celebrations for the fifth centenary of Christopher Columbus's voyage to America. New touring version of *Accidental Death of an Anarchist* produced by the Royal National Theatre, London.

1992 A completely new version of *Seventh: Steal a Little Less* performed by Franca alone opens in response to Italy's widening bribery scandals.

1993 *Dario Fo Meets Ruzante,* a reading of various extracts from Ruzante, the Venetian Renaissance actor-author whom Fo reveres above all others.

1994 Directs Rossini's *The Italian Girl in Algiers*. Franca stirs up controversy with a one-woman educational piece *Sex? Thank You! Don't Mind If I Do,* based on a book written by her son, Jacopo, entitled *Zen and the Art of Screwing.*

1995 Dario suffers a stroke at their seaside villa in Cesenatico. Suffers partial loss of memory and sight. Takes up painting once again. Makes a gradual, but almost complete recovery.

1997 The couple begin touring, but on a small scale, combining pieces of *Mistero Buffo* and *Sex? Thank You! Don't Mind If I Do. The Devil in Drag,* written and directed by Dario, with Franca in the leading part, opens in Sicily. Award of the Nobel Prize for Literature. The citation issued by the Swedish Royal Academy reads:

> Fo emulates the jesters of the Middle Ages in scourging authority and upholding the dignity of the downtrodden. For many years, Fo has been performed all over the world, perhaps more than any other contemporary dramatist, and his influence has been considerable. He, if anyone, merits the description of jester in the true meaning of the word. With a blend of laughter and gravity he opens our eyes to abuses and injustices in society, and also to the wider historical perspective in which they can be placed. Fo is an

extremely serious satirist with a multifaceted oeuvre. His independence and clear-sightedness have led him to take great risks, whose consequences he has been made to feel while at the same time experiencing enormous response from widely differing quarters.

Fo's strength is in the creation of texts that simultaneously amuse, engage and provide perspectives. As in *commedia dell'arte*, they are always open for additions and dislocations, continually encouraging the actors to improvise, which means that the audience is activated in a remarkable way. His is an oeuvre of impressive artistic vitality and range.

1998   *Free Marino! Marino Is Innocent!,* a militant piece denouncing Leonardo Marino who had alleged that Adriano Sofri was responsible for the murder of Inspector Calabresi. Retrospective art exhibition, 'Puppets with Rage and Feeling', mounted at Cesenatico, then touring.

1999   *The Holy Jester, Francis,* a largely respectful if idiosyncratic view of St Francis of Assisi, which wins Dario the thanks of the Vatican for being the only playwright to treat religious themes. Televised lecture on Leonardo da Vinci to celebrate the restoration of the *Last Supper.*

2000   Announces his candidature as Mayor of Milan; later withdrawn.

2001   Takes increasing interest in Green politics, including an appearance before the European parliament in Strasbourg to denounce bio-engineering.

2002   Retrospective season at the Piccolo Theatre in Milan. *My First Seven Years (plus a few more),* a memoir.

Plot

Accidental Death of an Anarchist is essentially an inquiry, or counter-inquiry, into a specific incident, so the plot does not feature the development of action or character: it is rather a challenge to a false version of events put about by authority figures. The momentum of the play is provided by the gradual increase of knowledge about the incident itself, and by the variety of farcical situations in which the challenge is mounted.

Act One, Scene One
The Maniac, who is never given a name, enters by the window, a device for focusing the audience's attention from the very outset on something which is more than stage furnishing. The window is at the heart of the investigation of the event which makes up the plot. The office into which the Maniac enters is in a police station. Inspector Bertozzo, whose office it is, comes in by the door, accompanied by a constable. The Maniac is obviously known to them, since they immediately produce a file with his previous convictions, all for acts of impersonation. The Maniac is no deranged individual with no control over his actions, but an obsessive character whose supposedly insane behaviour takes the form of a compulsive need to act out a variety of roles. He has managed to pass himself off as, among other things, a surgeon, a bishop and a psychiatrist but has spent some time in a mental hospital where he acquired a knowledge of law. The ensuing dialogue between the Inspector and the Maniac is an exercise in deliberately illogical, zany, nonsensical clowning, whose aim is to disorientate the ponderous police officer, but it also shows the Maniac's gifts for the improvised, off-the-cuff witticism and his ready inventiveness. He launches on the first of the many wild monologues he will deliver during the play, but the subject is not quite random,

since he ridicules judges for their arbitrary power and for their freedom to remain on the bench at an age when their clarity of mind is diminishing. He succeeds in exasperating the officers, but offers to get out of their way by throwing himself out of the window, a very obvious reference to the fate of the anarchist. They show him the door, and exit themselves to attend to some business.

Immediately afterwards, the Maniac returns to retrieve his papers, but finds the office deserted. He flicks through documents piled on the Inspector's desk, and throws some of the charge sheets out of the window, preserving others. In his search, he comes across one file which attracts his interest, the report made by a magistrate in charge of an investigation into the death in custody of an anarchist, never named in the play, suspected of involvement in a bombing outrage. The Maniac's examination is interrupted by a phone call from another inspector who, it transpires, is the officer who had been conducting the interrogation of the anarchist at the time of his mysterious death. The Maniac gathers from the Inspector news of the imminent arrival of another judge to revise the previous findings and to re-examine the police conduct in the case, but he drives the Inspector into a rage by pretending to speak for Bertozzo, and saying that the two of them find the problems facing the Inspector downright hilarious. To aggravate the offence, he conveys over the phone mocking messages and rude, derisive gestures supposedly from Bertozzo, and tells the Inspector that once his responsibilities for the anarchist's death have been uncovered, the best he can hope for is to be dispatched to a new posting in a remote, barren, unfriendly place like Huddersfield. Once off the phone, the Maniac seizes his opportunity, and begins to rehearse walks and poses which would help him pass himself off as the expected judge. He stuffs documents into a bag, but before he can get any further, Bertozzo returns. He is so anxious to get rid of the Maniac that he ignores his warning to watch out for an enraged Inspector out to wreak vengeance for his insolence. The Inspector turns up, and the scene closes with him throwing a punch at his colleague, Bertozzo.

Act One, Scene Two
The scene shifts to the Inspector's office on the fourth floor, the very place where the interrogation of the anarchist had taken place. The Maniac has already taken up his stance there when the Inspector and a constable enter. The self-confidence of the intruder disconcerts the officers, more so when he identifies himself as the judge entrusted with the new inquiry.

The initial exchanges contain the cut-and-thrust of comedy routines, but all the cutting and thrusting is done by the Maniac-judge. He insists on issuing a peremptory summons to the Superintendent, the senior officer in the police station. The Superintendent charges in, all indignant bluster at being given orders by an inferior officer, and the initial exchanges have once again the quality of the nonsensical comedy which arises from mistaken identity. Such mistakes over identity are of the essence in this farce. Once the Superintendent realises that he is in the presence of a high-ranking judge, he becomes more deferential, and attention is turned to the matter in hand. The Maniac picks up the use of the word 'raptus' (seizure) in an earlier report, and to establish what caused this sudden seizure asks the officers to re-enact their interrogation of the anarchist, beginning with the famous, intimidating entrance of the Superintendent. The policemen condemn themselves out of their own mouths, admitting in the re-enactment and in the words exchanged with the Maniac-judge that they had fabricated evidence to frame the anarchist for the bombing, or else lied about evidence they did not have so as to induce the 'raptus' which caused the alleged suicide.

Other hypotheses are produced in the cod replay of the events. There is no one explanation of the actual circumstances of the death advanced in the play. The satirical reconstruction aims to expose the behaviour of the police on the fatal night and to undermine the various, absurd explanations put forward by them to justify their actions. It transpires that the anarchist was threatened with dismissal over alleged, but unproved, implication in the bombing, was told that his alibi had collapsed, and was wrongly informed that his alleged accomplice in the outrage had confessed. The cowed policemen agree that all these allegations were false.

They fear that they will be made scapegoats, and that the politicians, having made use of them, will abandon them to the scorn of the press and public. They still balk at the Maniac's first suggested way out, by the same window as the anarchist.

At this stage, in the carefully planned structure of the play, there is a comic pause in the action as the characters, and the audience, are given a chance to digest the information they have been given. The police officers are left demoralised and depressed as they face their predicament, but the Maniac changes tack, tells them to cheer up since he has been fooling them. His plan, he now says, had been to make them realise the hopelessness of their position and encourage them to devise a more plausible explanation of what had been going on that night.

In the new version, the 'raptus' theory is jettisoned in favour of a more sophisticated tale which takes account of the gap of four hours between the onset of the 'raptus' and the fatal jump. The problem of what occurred in those hours is left to one side, as the Maniac persuades his charges that they had really been engaged on lulling the anarchist into a state of inner tranquillity. Other contradictory statements about his state of mind are almost incidentally produced – that he was completely calm or that he was nervously drawing on a cigarette – and as the play takes another turn towards pure farce, the Maniac gives a recapitulation of the allegations and facts so far established: the police had fabricated evidence, they had brought in an innocent and healthy man who had died while in their care, they had demoralised him with falsehoods, they had produced contradictory versions of what had led to his death. The only way they could redeem themselves, he suggests, is to show that they had behaved with humanity towards the increasingly desperate prisoner. Perhaps, he suggests, it had occurred to the Inspector that the anarchist was a railwayman, that he had remembered playing with trains as a child himself and that he had therefore given the anarchist's cheek a kindly pat. Or perhaps they had had the idea of a cheery sing-song, maybe involving an anarchist anthem. The act ends with the Maniac and officers lustily singing the song they had supposedly sung with the anarchist.

Act Two

There are no divisions into scenes given in Act Two, but there are certain natural breaks in the action. The curtain rises to reveal the performers in exactly the positions they had been in at the end of the previous act, still singing. The inquiry takes up from where it had left off.

It is agreed that the Superintendent had been absent at the crucial moment, but that the Inspector was one of the people present in the office throughout. The Maniac switches tone and mocks the police for the suggestion that they had been joking with the suspect. He goes off into a comic routine about depressives presenting themselves for interrogation in police stations for a good laugh. The police at this point begin to suspect that the Maniac is not as reliable a supporter as they might have imagined, but the discussion darkens, bringing up inconsistencies in the original reports. How plausible is the suggestion that the supposedly calm anarchist impulsively threw himself to his death just because insinuations were made against his fellow anarchist, Valpreda (unnamed) the dancer? The two were not on good terms, so could a few random insults to a man he did not like really drive him to suicide? The Maniac, tongue-in-cheek, raises the possibility that the anarchist had killed himself just to spite the police, but this is too much even for the slow-witted officers. Other anomalies are raised and dismissed: why was the window open on the coldest night of the year, how credible was the claim that a policeman showed his anxiety to save the anarchist by grabbing his foot as he rushed to the window, allegedly pulling off his shoe, when it was noted that the body had one shoe on either foot as it lay on the ground?

The decisive change of tone occurs when it is announced that a journalist has arrived to conduct an interview with the Inspector. The Maniac advises that she be allowed to come up, and offers to use his skill for disguise to stay in the office and give such help as is needed. He initially claims to be an officer from the forensic department of the police, but dresses himself in eye-patch, wooden leg and false moustache. His attitude towards the incisive questioning of the journalist disconcerts the whole group, since he is in turns helpful and obstructive. She asks the Inspector why he has the nickname Window-Straddler, and the Maniac intervenes, making fun of the question. Hoping to establish whether the body was still alive when it was ejected from the window, she asks about its trajectory, and the Maniac sides with her. She turns to the timing of the call for an ambulance, and he is back on the police side, but from the audience point of view, his intervention is irrelevant: the important point is that these questions are aired in public. He then raises the completely new possibility that the anarchist had been assaulted in the office and had lost his balance, falling out of the policemen's hands at the window while trying to regain his breath. Although the journalist's questions are unremittingly serious, the tone of farce is maintained in part by the Maniac's witticisms and in part by his loss of the glass eye, which is placed in a glass of water and drunk.

The tempo is now raised even further as various other points are brought up, such as the dismissal of the anarchist's alibi that he had been playing cards with old-age pensioners. This fact is an excuse for a digression on the position of retired folk who were suffering from industrial disabilities, but the final *coup de scène* is the arrival of Bertozzo. The disguise of the Maniac is now a game of double bluff: Bertozzo thinks he recognises him, while the others are afraid that Bertozzo will blow the Maniac's cover in front of the journalist. No scene is more pregnant with farcical potential. The Maniac adopts disguises of increasing extravagance, and the comic effect of the kicks and blows which rain on Bertozzo from colleagues is heightened by his total unawareness of what he has done to provoke this response.

Bertozzo is carrying a bomb, a replica of the one used for the explosion at the bank. The journalist enquires why the original bomb which failed to detonate was exploded rather than rendered harmless and examined, and why the information given by the neo-fascist infiltrators into the anarchist group was not acted on. Meantime, the Maniac himself takes on the role of *agent provocateur*, encouraging the journalist and advancing theories of his own as to why the police in their investigation of the bombing failed to follow up alternative leads involving Italian right-wing groups or international secret service agencies. As his eyepatch is removed and his wooden leg comes off, the Maniac delivers a speech on the importance of scandals in social democracy, explaining that they serve as safety valves. Political misdeeds can be blamed by the media on dubious individuals, not on deeper intrinsic flaws in the system. In this way, public anger is neutralised. Bertozzo's exasperation grows, but his colleagues become increasingly irritated with his efforts to reveal who the 'judge' is, and resort to such desperate measures as binding his mouth with tape. The Maniac himself replies by adopting an even more ludicrous disguise, as a bishop.

In desperation, Bertozzo produces a gun. He handcuffs all the police officers, the journalist and Maniac to a rail at the back of the stage, and is finally able to show them who the supposed judge really is. The Maniac replies by grabbing the bomb and threatening to set it off unless Bertozzo hands over the gun, which he does. The Maniac reveals that he has a tape-recording of the entire conversation, but since the others are all tied up and he has the bomb, there is little they can do. He announces his intention of sending the recording to the press so as to create a huge scandal, making Italy the equal of all other social democracies and forcing its citizens, since they 'are in the shit up to their necks', to go round with their heads held high.

The lights go out, there is an explosion and when the lights come on again it is found that the Maniac is no longer in the room. Downstairs in the courtyard, a group of people is seen to be gathering around a body which has fallen inexplicably from a window, but the people in the room are indifferent and the police instantly go on to auto-pilot and deny all knowledge of the events in which they had been participating. The journalist leaves to report her story and the policemen take keys out of their pockets and unlock their handcuffs. There is a knock on the door and a bearded newcomer, instantly recognisable as the actor who had played the Maniac, walks into the room. He is set upon by the policemen. They fall back in dismay when they find they have been victims of another double bluff, and the newcomer is a real judge, sent by Rome to conduct an inquiry into the death, accidental or otherwise, of the anarchist in police custody.

Commentary

The politics of farce

Carlo Goldoni, the eighteenth-century Venetian playwright,
wrote in his autobiography that he was 'born under the star
of comedy', and Dario Fo could make a comparable claim.
He brought to his theatre an innate talent for fun, a boundless
inventiveness, a taste for the nonsensical, a gift for zany
observation, a love of whimsy, a fantasy at home in the
realms of the absurd, a wayward glance at the affairs of men
and women that could have made him the equal of the great
writers of pure farce at any stage of theatrical history.
However, as he wrote in a study of the Italian comic actor,
Totò, no critic should attempt 'a historical or, above all,
critical, analysis of the technique of an actor if the actor in
question does not have a "poetic"; because it is in that, in the
themes through which it is developed, that "technique"
acquires breadth and meaning, becoming "style"' (*Totò*, p.9).
Fo, both as actor and author, possesses the style, the
technique and the theory and philosophy of theatre which
together constitute a 'poetic'. It is true that his unbounded,
instinctive creativity is often at odds with his 'poetic', but his
constant aim is to shape and structure his comic gifts so as to
forge a new kind of theatre which combines boisterous
laughter with a rage at injustice. In the process, he has
become one of the leading writers of political theatre of our
age.

However paradoxical it might seem for a writer whose
subject was politics, farce was his preferred medium, but a
wholly original style of farce which could be termed 'didactic
farce'. Most of the big political farces for which Fo is now
best known were written and performed in the years
following his break with 'bourgeois theatre' in 1968, but if
that year many new theatrical companies emerged all over

Europe to stage political theatre in which they proclaimed
their dedication to Marxism and the proletariat, the
difference was that 1968 was for Fo not a starting point but a
turning point in an already successful career. He had already
served a lengthy apprenticeship in theatre and given full proof
of his abilities both as actor and writer. From the outset, farce
was his favourite genre. At his debut as author with the four
one-act farces, linked under the umbrella title *Thieves,
Mannequins and Nude Women,* he told an interviewer: 'I
want to rehabilitate farce. Theatre critics have adopted the
habit of writing that an unsuccessful comedy "declines into
farce". Now I believe that farce is a noble – and modern –
genre of theatre.'

These plays were premiered in 1958, at the time when in
Paris Eugène Ionesco, Arthur Adamov and Samuel Beckett
were using farce to stage intellectual drama. Farce, long
despised by critics as vulgar entertainment, had come to be
viewed in the post-war period as the dramatic vehicle best
suited for the expression of a philosophic outlook known
simply as 'the Absurd', a philosophy which gave voice to the
sense of world-weariness, of blackness, of futility, of
pessimism over humanity which were widespread in Europe
after the final defeat of Nazism and Fascism. When his work
first appeared, various critics hailed Fo as the Italian Ionesco,
but he dissociated himself from this judgement and
proclaimed that his farce belonged to an older, popular
tradition. The others were writers of the avant-garde,
therefore in his eyes élitists, playing for a small audience of
intellectuals. He never had any sympathy with the avant-
garde. From the beginning, he wished to be numbered
among writers in the 'popular tradition'. This adherence
to a 'popular' culture, where the word 'popular' does not
have its acquired English meaning but its original sense
of 'belonging to the people', as distinct from the upper
classes, is indispensable to any understanding of Fo's
theatrical beliefs.

Although he developed complex views on what constitutes
such theatre and how it differs from 'bourgeois theatre', he
first stumbled on to it because it was a style of theatre the

Rame family had always practised. The second programme of
one-act farces, *Comica finale,* which he and Franca Rame
staged in 1958, were drawn from sketches and outline plot
which the Rame family-company had been performing for
popular audiences as they toured from venue to venue in
northern Italy. The tendency to find inspiration in the past, to
be a respecter of theatrical tradition and not an anarchic
iconoclast, a theatrical conservative rather than an
experimentalist, was to be a constant in Fo's career. However
radical and revolutionary were his politics, in matters
theatrical, Dario Fo can be viewed as a conservative, a man
who by preference inhabits tradition.

The characters on whom he most modelled himself after
1968 were two great comic figures – the medieval *giullare*
and the harlequin from *commedia dell'arte.* The word *giullare*
can be translated as 'jester', provided it is not taken in the
sense of 'court jester' but in the sense of the all-round
entertainer who performed to the people in the public places
of the cities. The figure makes his first appearance in one of
Fo's earliest plays, *Archangels Don't Play Pinball,* when
Lanky tells Blondie that his trade is to have people make a
fool of him. 'Do you remember who the *giullare* was?' he
asks. When she replies that he made kings laugh, Lanky
agrees but adds that since there are no more kings, he is
happy to make his friends in the bar laugh. After 1968,
Fo declared his plan to become the 'people's jester', and
there is something of the jester, and even more of the
harlequin, in the Maniac in *Accidental Death.* The jester
became the narrator-performer in *Mistero Buffo.*

In the tradition he chose, Fo awarded pride of place to the
lesser figures, the clowns, the jesters, the vaudeville
entertainers, the variety artistes, writers of farce, but above all
to those who spoke to and for the people. To this tradition,
Fo added the spice of satire and of the use of the grotesque
for satirical purposes. There was an element of, very gentle,
satire in those early one-act farces, but that element grew
stronger during his so-called 'bourgeois period' in the 1960s.
During that time, his plays were cast as comedy rather than
farce. The assumption has always been that farce is frivolous

and escapist, that it relies exclusively on the mechanisms of plot, that its humour derives from relentless pace and momentum, that it stages comic debacles and fiascos but casts no light on life, that it has no credibility or value outside its own closed world, and that even in that world it requires a high level of suspension of belief. Comedy, on the other hand, has always been viewed as having a sophistication lacking in farce, since it contains some form of character development and offers some form of intellectual challenge beneath the light-hearted romp. Comedy was, then, accorded a respectable place in a hierarchy of dramatic forms, below tragedy, but well above mere farce. Fo challenged this order, but in his 'bourgeois' period, comedy was his medium. In any case, the distinction between the two genres is delicate and ethereal. For Fo, there was little real break between comedy and farce. 'The choice of writing a comedy involves the choice of a more complex structure than that of farce. While the farce is based from beginning to end on a theatrical mechanism which employs a single device, comedy has a structure articulated according to the storyline, so the devices can be multiple.'

Fo never eschewed slapstick humour, either in comedy or farce. His plays all contain passages of raucous, rumbustious knockabout, of surreal fancy, of outrageous fantasy which serve no purpose either in terms of plot or politics. Even in his most earnestly political period, he found it hard to discipline his own inventiveness when he discovered that certain scenes aroused delighted laughter. He was happy to provide a good night out, even when he wished also to develop some idea on the political situation of his own day. The 1961 play, *He Who Steals a Foot is Lucky in Love*, is an attack on corruption in the building trade at a time when the award of public contracts in Italy was arousing suspicion, but discussions between constructors are interrupted by moments when they squirt drinks into each others' faces.

However, the fact that his plots concern public situations meant that Italy's censors followed his development with close interest. At that time, all scripts had to be submitted to Rome for approval, but this move was futile in the case of a

writer like Fo, who changed his texts continually during
rehearsals and even during the run. Outraged censors took to
attending his performances with little torches which they used
to peer at the approved text they had in their hands and to
note any changes from dialogue spoken on stage. They were
especially upset by a play entitled *He Had Two Pistols and
White and Black Eyes* (1960), in which Dario played both the
part of a priest who has lost his memory and a bandit on the
run. The action unfolds in a psychiatric hospital run by
doctors dressed as clerics, a situation which the censors
interpreted, rightly, as an image of Italy governed by the
Christian Democrats. The image of insanity, of a world
upside down, recurs in Fo's theatre. In *Accidental Death of an
Anarchist,* the Maniac is the standard-bearer of sanity and
logic.

Satire is of the essence in Fo's poetics of theatre. The irony
or ridicule which are intrinsic to satire remove all solemnity
from its target, leaving the emperor with no clothes and
therefore undeserving of respect. To say that the leaders of
the Soviet Union in the days of Stalin were cruel and
hypocritical is merely an attack. To portray them, as does
George Orwell in *Animal Farm,* as pigs, who lead the revolt
of the other animals only to assume themselves all the
privileges of the humans they had ousted, is satire at its
highest. Satire is rarely refined, gentle or sophisticated, but
can be violent, brutal, pitiless or even tragic. Fo expressed his
admiration for Jonathan Swift's bitter satire, *A Modest
Proposal,* where the writer suggested that the problem of
poverty and hunger in Ireland could be relieved by the
reintroduction of cannibalism. The children of the poor, Swift
pointed out in his satire, were well fed and healthy until
about the age of three when their mothers stopped breast-
feeding them. After that, food being short, they tended to
grow more sickly and unhealthy. Now, suggested Swift,
suppose that we sell these infants to the wealthy diners in
England and France who could be persuaded to regard infant
flesh as a delicacy. The families would thus receive some form
of income, they would be freed of a burden they could not
support, while the children themselves would not have to put

up with the privations and misery of poverty. Fo regarded this satire as among the most perfect ever penned, and used it to illustrate his central point. He was short with those who objected to violence, or even obscenity, in satirical writing, provided they were not ends in themselves. He had no truck with gratuitous violence, and no liking for the merely lascivious, but if they served the purpose of seizing attention, of making people concentrate on a wider point, these means could be accepted. In a one-act play, *The Boss's Funeral* (1969), he focuses on workplace deaths in Italy. To drive home his point, a butcher, complete with knives and axe, appears at the end of the action, holding in his arms a baby goat which he is about to slaughter. In the debate, Fo asks his spectators to consider why they are horrified at the sight of the slaughter of an animal and so indifferent to the killings which occur routinely in the industrial process. (The goat was not injured.)

For Fo, satire, real satire, is part of the mindset which produces tragedy: without the sense of tragedy, satire is mere caricature, or the relaxed jokiness which will allow the supposed object of, for example, cartoon satire to request of the cartoonist copies of the work in which he is supposedly slated. A good-hearted caricature which lampoons a politician by giving him a big nose or flappy ears is not satire but fluffy humour.

> It is nearly a mechanical constant: where the satirical form does not have tragedy as its counterpart, the whole thing is transformed into clowning. Tragedy as drama of hunger, as terror and refusal of violence in all senses, the problem of human respect, the problem of dignity and of the quality of life, the problem of the relationship with death, the problem of love, of sexuality – this is the real catalyst of comic satire. (*Dialogo provocatorio*, p.5)

This combination of seemingly tasteless satire and tragedy reaches its highest point in *Accidental Death of an Anarchist*. To make a farce out of a tragedy which cost an innocent man his life, in which the people who were responsible for that death were the forces of law and order, is an unusually bold

act. Fo is not, plainly, laughing at the death of the
unfortunate Pino Pinelli, but does not shy away from
arousing laughter as a means of compelling people to
meditate deeply on the human responsibilities for that death.

Farce seemed to him the most effective means of provoking
thought. On more than one occasion, he said that his aim was
to provoke 'laughter with anger'. It is a unique combination.
There is no shortage of playwrights who have used theatre as
a forum for the debate of political subjects. Perhaps the
greatest of political playwrights of the twentieth century was
the German Bertolt Brecht (1898–1956), but while there are
comic scenes in Brecht, his plays cannot be described as either
comedy or farce. *The Resistible Rise of Arturo Ui* (1957, but
written in 1941) is a savage satire on the rise of Hitler, where
the Hitler figure is a small-time thug in Chicago who flatters
and deceives fellow-gangsters until he has attained power, at
which point he has them murdered. One of the most comic
scenes shows Arturo taking lessons from an actor who has
fallen on hard times and who teaches him how to march,
parade himself in public, gesticulate and deliver oratory.
Brecht preferred drama to comedy, but developed a theory of
'alienation effect' which was designed to prevent spectators
from becoming so involved in the fiction they were watching
that they lost the detachment needed to allow them to judge
the politics debated in the play.

Fo too thought deeply about this problem but while he was
deeply influenced by Brecht, he was also critical and believed
that popular theatre and farce already provided the means to
prevent this level of undesirable involvement. He had no
intention of producing high-minded, tedious theatre which
could not hold people's attention. Entertainment, enjoyment,
pleasure were among the goals of theatre, and it was certainly
his intention to provide them *as well,* but escapist theatre, the
equivalent of the TV sit-com, theatre which aimed to purvey
only thoughtless entertainment was not for him. Popular
theatre of whatever kind, he noted, had an in-built
mechanism which gave the aware playwright the chance of
attaining 'alienation effect', or the detachment which stopped
undue absorption in a pure fiction. The mechanism is the

absence of the 'fourth wall', that invisible barrier which divides stage from stalls. The fourth wall was the imaginary divide across which there could be no conversation: in this tradition, actors remained in part, as King Lear or Falstaff, never engaging in debate with the paying public. In popular theatre, this convention was not respected. In music hall, for example, performers would engage in repartee with people in the front rows; in pantomime, the principal actors would emerge at the end of the play to read out names of groups in attendance that night, or to do a stand-up routine. Fo used this freedom in his theatre.

In addition, he believed that farce was a device which prevented 'catharsis'. The term 'catharsis' first appears in the discussion of tragedy in Aristotle's *Poetics,* written around 330 BC. The exact meaning has been subject to endless debate, but the most common interpretation is that 'catharsis' is a medical metaphor whose meaning is, broadly, 'cleansing'. A play, in other words, arouses certain sentiments, notably pity and fear, with the aim of purging and eliminating them from the intellectual and emotional systems of spectators. For this very reason, Fo was hostile to any technique that attained the effect of catharsis. In one of his discussions with the audience after a performance of *Accidental Death of an Anarchist,* he said:

> The people does not use the dramatic methods of the aristocracy, the one which grabs at heart and guts, but attempts to get there by a violent moment of laughter. Because laughter really does remain at the bottom of the mind, leaving sediment which cannot be wiped off. Because laughter helps avoid one of the worst dangers, which is catharsis. That is, whenever someone cries, he frees himself of pain [. . .] There is no need to add that if there really is a divide between aristocratic theatre and the people's comic theatre, it has to do with the comic spirit of the one as against the pompous seriousness of the other. Now, the fact that this play contains a grotesque element, is quite deliberate. We do not wish to free from indignation people who come along – we say so at the end. We want their anger to stay inside them, to remain there and not be let go, we want it to become active, we want to force

people to reason about the time we find ourselves in, and we want them to carry all this forward into the struggle. (*Compagni senza censura*, pp.189–90)

Fo's aim was quite the reverse of catharsis. His theatre sought to provoke debate, to arouse feelings, to challenge received ideas and invite people to consider new points of view. His audience was invited to take part in a political 'struggle', a term much in vogue in those troubled years. Dario Fo was advocating Marxist revolution, and it is no service to him to dilute the beliefs he held in those years. As a theatre-maker, he had no desire to hold people's interest just for the duration of a show, only to see them forget all that had been presented to them once they put on their coats and exited into the night. His desire was that they left the theatre changed. Laughter is, in this view, a mechanism for triggering thought. Dario was fond of quoting Molière to the effect that while tragedy was emotionally comforting, laughter was defiant. Laughter is the identifying mark of humanity, since in laughter the human being becomes fully conscious of his own potential, of his individuality and of his ability to assert his autonomy from convention and rule. 'Laughter denotes a critical awareness; it signifies imagination, intelligence and a rejection of all fanaticism. In the scale of human evolution, we have first *homo sapiens,* then *homo faber* and then finally *homo ridens*, and this last is always the most difficult to subdue or make conform' (*Tricks of the Trade*, p.109).

Part of the reason for his admiration of Vladimir Mayakovsky (1893–1930), the Russian poet of the Bolshevik revolution who ended up committing suicide in dismay at the course of Soviet government, was that he shared with him a common vision of the potential of theatre. Fo edited a collection of Mayakovsky's writings, which included the quotation:

Since I consider theatre to be an arena capable of reflecting political debates, I try to find a form capable of resolving these problems. First of all, I state that theatre is an arena and secondly a matter of performance, that is, once again, a joyful polemical arena.

Fo added his own comment, which may be taken as a statement of his belief:

> A theatre, then, to awaken consciences, not to amuse them, to
> stimulate doubts and discussions, not to perpetrate
> commonplaces; a theatre to which I feel extremely close, one
> directly linked to reflection, to the political analysis of society and
> one which takes its inspiration from it to modify it by means of
> the fantastic, the ironic, the grotesque (the very forms of theatre).
> (*Messaggi*, p.141)

Turbulence and disorder: Italy in 1969

Few plays have had such a varied afterlife as Dario Fo's
Accidental Death of an Anarchist. It has been performed all
over the world, presented on some stages as an all-purpose
protest play, but viewed in other quarters as whimsical,
knockabout farce. Perhaps only Jonathan Swift's *Gulliver's
Travels*, another work originally written as a satire on the
politics of his age but then taken as playful fantasy fit for
children, has suffered, or enjoyed, a comparable fate.
The oddity of the fate of Fo's play is that it was written in a
precise context and represented a response to a specific event
in the turbulent Italy of the late sixties. Far from being a
purely escapist, uproarious farce, it was conceived as a hard-
hitting political drama, designed to arouse anger over the
death in custody of an innocent man in 1969, and over a
wider crime against democracy committed by the powers-
that-be in Italy. The official politics of Italy in the sixties were
dominated by the Christian Democratic party, the principal
party of government, and by the Italian Communist party.
The fact that the alternative party was communist, not
democratic socialist as elsewhere in Europe, aroused alarm in
certain quarters and meant that there were sinister, covert
forces at work inside the country whose aim was either to
keep the communists out of government at any price, or to
topple the democratic government and to introduce some
non-democratic, possibly totalitarian or fascist, style of rule.

Here we move into territory which it is impossible to chart with total accuracy. Historians and pundits talk of an 'Italy of the mysteries', an Italy whose direction was determined by cabals, mafias, masonries, unaccountable forces, faceless societies, groups whose composition was unknown to the public at large.

Italy in those years was shaken by a series of scandals which in their dimensions were without parallel elsewhere. Some were the humdrum, if regrettable, consequences of the quest for favours in a regime of uninterrupted one-party rule, but others had more sinister connotations. These latter include the illegal activities of the American oil companies, uncovered not by some left-wing fanatic but by a committee of the American Senate chaired by Senator Church, and the corrupt and corrupting behaviour of the Lockheed company in the mid-1970s, when the company was involved in systematically bribing politicians. The English historian Denis Mack Smith writes:

> A report to the American Congress revealed that in recent years [that is, the years leading to the 1975 general elections] more than a hundred million dollars reached Italy from America to support the anticommunist cause. Most of this money went to the Christian Democrat party but some was sent directly to the Italian secret services who had close links to neo-fascism. How much other American money was funnelled through the covert military organization of Gladio cannot be known, but more than once the Italian government imposed a veto on disclosure to parliament about the financing of mysterious groups suspected of involvement with right-wing terrorism.

Operation Gladio, whose existence was only revealed in 1990, was part of a Europe-wide network of underground organisations, codenamed Stay Behind, whose original task was to act as a focus for resistance in the event of some Soviet invasion of western Europe, but whose activities were more suspect. Acting in conjunction with the CIA, it had unofficial arms dumps around the country. There were other shadowy groups, like the P2 masonic lodge, which advocated regime change in Italy, pronounced itself in favour of a strong presidential system and did not shy away from the use of systematic corruption. Several police investigations have linked P2 to right-wing terrorism, specifically to the bombing of the Italicus train in 1974. Its Grand Master, Licio Gelli, received a heavy jail sentence for his alleged part in the 1980 explosion at the Bologna railway station which left eighty-five people dead.

Taken together with other covert groups, these organisations were viewed by many commentators both then and subsequently as constituting what was known as the 'second state', 'the alternative state', the 'state within a state', or more generally as 'Italy of the mysteries'. There were two separate attempts at a coup d'état in Italy within a few years of each other, the first led by General De Lorenzo in 1964 and the second headed by the 'Black Prince' Juan Valerio Borghese in 1970. The fact that there were elements of comic opera to the execution of both ventures does not lessen their seriousness. The first was unobserved by the general public at the time, but was revealed by the *Espresso* magazine in 1967 when it added to the general sense of unease in society, and the second was called off when it was under way, seemingly because it was raining in Rome and the troops stationed at street corners were uncomfortable. The attempts at instituting undemocratic governments seemed to be part of a wider strategy at the time. Spain was still under Franco, Portugal ruled by the heirs of Salazar and the democratic government in Greece had been overthrown in 1967 by a coup d'état led by military officers, the so-called 'Colonels'. The international objective was perceived by the left as the establishment of right-wing regimes all around the Mediterranean, and the means adopted inside Italy were what became known as a 'strategy of tension'. The nature of the strategy was clear. The use of indiscriminate killing was expected to create a climate of panic in Italy which would lead to a popular demand for strong repressive measures and would eventually cause the electorate, in revulsion at the monstrosities being perpetrated on the streets or in fear of the continuation of a terror campaign, to rise against the current rulers and call for the installation of a new regime, headed by a totalitarian 'strong man'. The bombing of the bank which preceded the events outlined in the play was one such incident.

By 1969, there were at least the beginnings of the terrorist groups which would sow havoc in the streets of Italy throughout the seventies and early eighties. The problem for the security forces was that they faced a twin threat from 'opposing extremisms' of left and right, the left preaching revolution, the right working to bring about a coup d'état. To a large extent each fed on a fear, perhaps paranoid, of the other. The first terrorist attacks occurred in the sixties, and some estimates put the number of attacks in 1969 as high as 150. The neo-fascists were historically first in the field of terror, but the revolutionary Marxist left followed. Several of the early offences, as was the case with the massacre in Milan which sparked off the events described in *Accidental Death of an Anarchist,* were in fact perpetrated by neo-fascists but ascribed to left-wing terror groups, in accordance with the logic of the strategy of tension.

It was August 1970 before the Red Brigades made their first public appearance when leaflets bearing their name were scattered outside the Sit-Siemens plant in Milan, but dissident collectives, often preaching violence at least in theory, had made their entrance sooner. All over Europe and North America, the 1960s were a time of upheaval, of convulsions, of innovations, of the overturning of established beliefs and practices in politics, in the arts, in morals. If the sixties are now associated with imprecise memories of joyful, anarchic groups like the hippies, with their preaching of 'flower power', free love and drug-taking, there was another strand to street activity in that decade. In the sixties, students took to the streets to protest against the politics pursued by their elders and to demand new courses of action. In the 'hot autumn' of 1969 in Italy, student militants seemed on the point of linking up with striking trade unionists. The contract of the steelworkers was due for renegotiation in September and the preceding months were marked by strikes, lock-outs and episodes of industrial action which started in the factory but spilled on to the streets. The centre of this unrest was the Fiat works in Turin. On 2 September, Fiat suspended some

25,000 workers, who replied on 18 November with a 'trial' of the owners and managers of the car plant. Violence was becoming routine. In the early months of 1969, several bombs exploded in Milan, the most serious going off at the Fiat pavilion in the Fiera di Milano, leaving nineteen people injured. On 9 August, bombs were planted on eight trains, causing injuries to ten people. In November, during demonstrations in Milan in the course a one-day general strike, a policeman, Antonio Annarumma, was killed. President Saragat went on television to denounce the strikers, although no one was ever convicted of the offence and it later appeared likely that he was killed by a police car.

Italy in 1969 was a divided, turbulent country, with the middle classes and established political parties, both on the left and the right, gazing in horror at developments in culture, industry, in society and in politics they could not understand and could not control. It was in this context that there occurred the most appalling crime of 1969, and the event which would shape Italian life for decades ahead.

Piazza Fontana

On the 12 December 1969, a bomb went off in the Banca dell'Agricoltura in Piazza Fontana in the centre of Milan. It was at 4.30 on a Friday afternoon, and the bank was filled with weekend customers and with farmers and dealers who had been attending the weekly market. The device was packed with high explosives, and was designed to cause the maximum injury and loss of life. Sixteen people were killed, immediately or died subsequently in hospital, and a further ninety received injuries of greater or lesser gravity.

There were other explosions in Italy that day. One hour previously, a bag containing explosives was discovered in another bank in Milan, but it failed to detonate. Astonishingly, or suspiciously, the police blew the bomb up rather than having it rendered harmless by bomb-disposal experts. This decision, which came to look increasingly suspicious in the light of subsequent developments, meant that a potentially important piece of evidence which could have led investigators to the manufacturers of the device was destroyed. Was this merely thoughtless incompetence? In Rome, three devices exploded. One had been left in a bank, another near the tomb of the Unknown Soldier in the Altare della Patria in Piazza Venezia, and a third near the Risorgimento Museum in the same square. All three went off causing injuries to police guards and passers-by, but none of any great seriousness.

It was Piazza Fontana which caused shock then and whose after-effects continued to be felt for decades to come. There were subsequent terrorist atrocities in Italy – the massacre of eight people in Brescia in 1974, the blowing-up of the Italicus train in the same year, and the explosion in the Bologna railway station in 1980 – which caused greater loss of life, but none had quite the impact of Piazza Fontana. The respected philosopher, Norberto Bobbio, has written that 'the degeneration of our democratic system began with Piazza Fontana'. Another writer, Giampiero Mughini, made the comment: 'The fact is that in December 1969 an order, a moral order above all, was sundered. There began a saga of bombings whose authorship is unknown, but of which it is known that they come from close at hand, mainly from desperate, fanatical groupings of "blacks" [that is, fascists] out for revenge for the 25 April 1945 [the day the war ended in Italy].' Giorgio Bocca, journalist and author, referred to the massacre as the event 'which changed the lives of generations'. The events of that day have been analysed minute by minute, books have been written on the subject, TV programmes dedicated to it, newspaper columnists have gone over it in detail, parliamentary commissions have examined it and trials, counter-trials, appeals and varied courts hearings with different groupings of accused have scrutinised the questions of guilt and responsibility, but it is still impossible to say if the truth about the matter has been fully extricated from the web of lies spun around it by policemen, judges, politicians, army generals and journalists. Or ever will be.

It did not look that way to readers of newspapers in the

days immediately following the bombing. With suspicious speed, the police and the magistrates felt able to announce that anarchist circles were responsible for its planning and execution. Hundreds of anarchists were rounded up. One of the first was Giuseppe (Pino) Pinelli, arrested before nightfall on the day of the outrage, taken to the police station in Milan, subjected to seventy-two hours of futile interrogation in the office of Inspector Calabresi, before 'falling' to his death on the night of 15–16 December. The word 'falling' must remain for ever in inverted commas, to mark the unsettled dispute which raged for years afterwards concerning the circumstances in which he met his death. The one undoubted fact is that around midnight on the 15 December his body was seen plunging from the window of Calabresi's office on to the courtyard of the police station. Was he pushed from the window, did he fall, did he jump, was he already dead when his body was thrown to the ground? Was his death suicide, and thus possibly an admission of guilt, was he so badly manhandled, or even tortured, inside the office that he expired, was he made to sit on the windowsill from which he fell in a sort of accident, or was he otherwise killed? Was there a police cover-up, and who was involved in it? The death of Pinelli is the basis – it can hardly be called inspiration – for Dario Fo's play. Pinelli was the anarchist of the title, but the other principal characters, like the Inspector and the journalist, are also based on the people involved in the unfolding story.

The arrests continued, with the other principal victim of the miscarriage of justice, Pietro Valpreda (1933–2002), another anarchist, arrested on the day Pinelli met his death. If the justice system was to reveal itself intolerably slow, the press moved with indecent haste to attribute blame. The communist daily, *L'Unità,* had no hesitation in referring to Valpreda as the 'monster'. Years later, Valpreda would recall how at the end of an interrogation session in Rome with the judge Vittorio Occorsio (himself gunned down by neo-fascist terrorists in 1976), he was brought into a room filled with press photographers who shouted to him, 'Head up, monster!' On 17 December, Milan's main daily newspaper, the *Corriere della Sera,* ran an article headlined 'The Propaganda of Terror'.

> In the space of four days, the agonising mystery surrounding the massacre of Piazza Fontana and the other attacks of last Friday has been resolved. The authorities have reached precise, concrete convictions on the environment in which the ferocious plan of destruction and the motives which armed the hands of the bombers was thought up and brought to fruition. The crime found food and nourishment in those anarchist or anarchoid circles and groups where the preaching of hatred and subversion, already in the past translated into practice, became a violent obsession. One of the most active of protagonists of this blood-stained apocalypse, the ballet-dancer Pietro Valpreda, 37, was reported by the police to the magistrates for complicity in massacres. In him, the man who was responsible for the atrocious end of fourteen people has been uncovered. The crime has now a precise physiognomy, the criminal has a face.

The problem was that the public were given the wrong face and told to blame the wrong ideological group. The anarchists were innocent, as Fo set out to assert in his play. Neither Valpreda nor Pinelli was involved in the massacre.

The anarchist, Pino Pinelli

Pino Pinelli was invariably referred to both in police reports and in newspaper articles as 'the anarchist, Pinelli'. Few other men have ever been identified exclusively in terms of their political affiliation, but it is senseless to question it now, especially since the description was accurate. A native of Milan, Pinelli was a railwayman by trade and an anarchist by conviction. Aged forty-one at the time of his arrest, he was no more than a pawn cruelly and callously used in a game whose rules he could not possibly have understood. He received his 'moral compensation' from Dario Fo, who crusaded on his behalf, but in his play, Fo does not show pity towards Pinelli, not because he felt none, but because his aim was to arouse anger among the living over Pinelli's fate and over the plight of Italian democracy. By all accounts, Pinelli was a quiet family man, largely self-taught, who lived with his wife and two daughters in a poorly furnished flat in one of the poorer districts of Milan. He was an enthusiast for Esperanto, believing that the use of a common language would lessen the risk of international conflict. An uncompromising believer in non-violence, it seems he was not particularly sympathetic to the permissive sexual mores preached in the sixties. No one could have predicted that this private man would be labelled a 'monster' by the right-wing press or that he would become a martyr for the left, his name carried on placards during demonstrations. For the writer Camilla Cederna, his name became a 'common remorse, a source of deep unease, and finally an accusation'.

There were six police officers in Calabresi's office when Pinelli met his death, but there was also a group of journalists in the courtyard below. Extracts from the evidence the policemen later gave were incorporated by Fo into the play, with the satirical aim of ridiculing the inconsistencies in the differing accounts given at different times in their attempts to exculpate themselves. Some of the most farcical points in the play were actually lifted straight from the minutes of the inquiry. The statement that Pinelli's shoe ended up in the hands of one of the officers who made a lunge to prevent Pinelli throwing himself from the window was made by Vito Panessa, a constable. The difficulty was that the journalists below saw that Pinelli was wearing both shoes when he hit the ground, leading Fo to suggest to his fictional policemen that they are home and dry if they can prove that Pinelli was a triped. Similarly, the fact that the window was open at the height of winter was hard to explain. If it had been shut, why were several robust officers unable to restrain one exhausted suspect in a confined space?

These were details, but the central fact was that the police provided several contradictory versions of the death. The chief of police, Marcello Guida, announced that the death was suicide, and an implicit admission of guilt. He added, 'I swear that we did not kill him,' a statement which aroused suspicions that he was protesting too much. The preliminary investigation was conducted by the magistrate Giovanni

Caizzi, who concluded that the evidence pointed to 'an accidental death', a conclusion Fo gratefully used as his title. There was a second inquiry conducted by another judge, Antonio Amati, which reverted to the suicide verdict. The inquiry was conducted in secret, which prevented Pinelli's widow from being represented, as happened also with the first post-mortem, when she was debarred from appointing her own doctor. The autopsy concluded that the death was due to the fall, not to any prior event.

The evidence which began to trickle out simply did not support this verdict, and in November 1971 Pinelli's widow raised a case against the police. The autopsy confirmed that Pinelli had bruises on his neck consistent with blows. The inquiry was conducted by Gerardo D'Ambrosio, a magistrate who would later be admired all over Italy for his part in exposing the business-politics corruption scandal known as Tangentopoli (Bribesville). D'Ambrosio published his findings in 1975, concluding that Pinelli had neither killed himself nor been killed but had been the victim of a *malore attivo,* an 'active faintness', a condition previously unknown to medical science. This loss of balance provoked the fall, and allowed the magistrate to reject the hypotheses of suicide or of the defenestration of a dead body. The police were acquitted and that part of the case closed.

By the time D'Ambrosio reached his verdict, Calabresi too was dead, assassinated outside his home in Milan on 17 May 1972. Calabresi had become the central personage in the unofficial inquiry into the death of Pinelli, and the main suspect for those who believed that Pinelli had been murdered. Luigi Calabresi was suspected of fascist sympathies and was already a *bête noire* for the left before Piazza Fontana. Much was made of the fact that he had been a guest of the CIA in America in 1966, that he was on friendly terms with General De Lorenzo who led the botched putsch in 1964 and that he had been used by American espionage agents to escort their men around Rome. Calabresi had been involved in the inquiry into one of the earliest of the bombings, at the Fiat pavilion in the Milan Fair on 25 April 1969. As would happen with Piazza Fontana, he immediately blamed 'elements of the left', and eight anarchists and communists were arrested. The trial was held in 1971, but the case collapsed, and several of the accused stated that Calabresi had beaten them up to extract confessions. It was he who declared to *La Stampa* newspaper that Piazza Fontana was the work of 'left-wing extremists'.

One of the most prominent of the New Left formations was Lotta Continua (Continual Struggle), who also published a daily newspaper. The paper ran a campaign against Calabresi, openly blaming him for the death of Pinelli. On 14 February 1970, the paper published the first of a series of satirical, insinuating and wickedly funny cartoons which excoriated Calabresi. One depicted a tender domestic scene with Calabresi playing in seeming innocence with his daughter, until the eye falls on the child's toy, a guillotine. Another has a montage of Calabresi standing before the door of a train at a station and a passenger turning to him and asking – 'What are you doing? Pushing?' The most devastating showed an office with the nameplate 'Calabresi' and a suspect entering gingerly, wearing a parachute. It was *Lotta Continua* which coined, or at least popularised, the nickname for Calabresi, Officer Window-Straddler. They carried the allegation, deadly in the circumstances, that one of Calabresi's interrogation techniques was to force a suspect to sit on the window ledge of his office, four storeys above the courtyard. Fo cheerfully made use of this information in his play.

He also drew attention to the fact that Calabresi developed a nervous twitch, perhaps due to the fact that he felt isolated and abandoned by his colleagues. The *Lotta Continua* campaign undermined his increasingly fragile psyche, and he decided to raise a legal action against the newspaper and its editor, Pio Baldelli, for criminal libel, still a crime under Italian law. The trial opened on 9 October 1970, but from the outset it seemed that Calabresi, not Baldelli, was in the dock, and that the issue was not libel but the responsibilities for Piazza Fontana and the death of Pino Pinelli. By this time, Dario Fo's play was in production, and the script was adapted performance by performance to take account of the

day's developments. The trial was particularly tortuous.
Calabresi's lawyer challenged the judge, who was removed
from the case and had his salary stopped. On 14 May,
Calabresi's bodyguard was declared unnecessary and
removed, and three days later he was murdered.

The mysterious death of the left-wing publisher,
Giangiacomo Feltrinelli, and the first Red Brigade operation
occurred around that time, so the climate was tense. The left
had to take a stance over terrorism. The journal *Lotta
Continua* followed a particularly tortuous line of reasoning in
which they deplored the use of terror for political ends, but
rejoiced more or less openly over the death of Calabresi.
Some of its journalists ended up in the dock on the odd
charge of 'apology for crime'. The editorial on the day after
the murder said that it was necessary to repeat 'the truth that
we have always spoken loud and clear – that Calabresi was a
murderer'. However it continued, 'political murder is not the
decisive weapon for the emancipation of the masses,' before
concluding 'but these considerations can by no means induce
us to deplore the Calabresi killing, an act in which the
exploited acknowledge their own will to justice'. Dario Fo
and his company were no more forgiving. In a note to the
play, signed not by Fo personally but by the co-operative of
which he was leading member, it was stated that the play was
intended to accompany the trial of Pio Baldelli and the legal
inquiry prompted by Licia Pinelli's complaint to the
magistrates. These inquiries were postponed and later
definitively suspended 'on account of the non-accidental
death of the actor'. It was a brutal epitaph for Calabresi.

As a coda, it could be added that this was not the last word
on the whole catastrophic business, nor the last intervention
of Fo into the case. No one was arrested at the time for the
murder, but in 1988 Leonardo Marino alleged to the police
that he had been driver of the car used to carry Calabresi's
killers, and that the guilty men were Adriano Sofri, Ovidio
Bompressi and Giorgio Pietrostefani. All four men had been
members of Lotta Continua in the seventies, and Sofri had
gone on to become a noted writer, political commentator and
member of the liberal establishment. The case became another

cause célèbre, and another disgrace for the Italian justice system. Strong doubts were cast on the allegations made by Marino, but the case proceeded through the hierarchy of Italian courts, with verdicts, findings, appeals and retrials, before being completed at the ninth attempt in October 2000. Sofri is currently in jail, in spite of widespread belief that he is innocent. Another library of books has appeared on this case, with the historian Carlo Ginzburg comparing the conduct of the trial to Renaissance witch trials, and Umberto Eco, Vincenzo Consolo, Dacia Maraini and many other writers in Italy, Germany, Spain and France proclaiming their belief in the innocence of the convicted men and calling for their release. Dario Fo has been as fully involved in this case as he was in the cases of Pinelli and of Valpreda. The first work he wrote after receiving the Nobel prize was entitled *Free Marino! Marino Is Innocent!,* a bitter, biting satirical attack on the evidence given by Leonardo Marino. Fo's involvement with the tragic events unleashed by the Piazza Fontana bombing is not at an end.

The characters

The Maniac
The Maniac, uniquely in this play, has no counterpart among the real participants in the events surrounding the bombing at Piazza Fontana, or the subsequent interrogation and death of Pino Pinelli. He is both a product of Dario Fo's imagination and a figure with deep roots in the Italian tradition of theatre. Fo's characters exist as a function of the situation they serve or of the actions they perform. 'Our theatre, unlike the theatre of Pirandello or Chekhov, is not bourgeois theatre, not the theatre of characters who recount their own stories, their own moods which then become the "key" to a mechanical conflict. It was always our concern to follow another line, the "situation" line' (*Teatro politico*, p.10).

The Maniac figure has antecedents in the Italian theatrical tradition of *commedia dell'arte*. This style of theatre, which flourished approximately from the mid-sixteenth to the mid-

eighteenth centuries, put the actor not the writer at the heart
of the play-making process, required the actors to wear masks
to denote the characters they were playing, was based on
improvisation rather than on fully written scripts, and used
plots featuring not individuals but stock characters. The most
celebrated of such characters was Arlecchino, Harlequin in
English, who wore a half-mask over the eyes and upper
mouth, and who had a long, hooked nose. His dress consisted
of the now famous, multi-coloured, lozenged costume.
Harlequin, and the viewpoint espoused by the Harlequin
character, was fundamental to Fo's style of comedy. At the
Venice Biennale in 1985, he put on a show dedicated to the
evolution of Harlequin but his interpretation of Harlequin
had nothing in common with the dandified, prettified version
which appears on the lids of chocolate boxes, or even with
the gentler comic version which made its appearance in the
late-eighteenth century and which still occasionally turns up
in British pantomime. Arlecchino first appeared as a servant
character, notable for his insatiable greed, and displaying
enormous physical and moral versatility in his drive for self-
preservation. The most famous example of this Arlecchino
appeared in Carlo Goldoni's eighteenth-century play,
Harlequin, Servant of Two Masters.

Fo dissented from this vision of Harlequin, which he spoke
of as 'castrated'. His Harlequin was a bestial figure, given to
obscene display, riven by greeds, and liable to be carried away
by his own appetites, sexual lusts as well as hunger. If he was
a forerunner of the clown, he was also wily, devious,
scheming, unscrupulous, irreverent and untrustworthy.
Speaking of his Venice show, Fo stated, 'This Harlequin is in
some ways the opposite of the one we know. The Harlequin
born of the inventiveness of the medieval clowns is an
anarchic character *ante litteram*, who has no sympathy with
current moral rules, the rules of authority [. . .] he is a free
spirit, a prevaricating, violent and scurrilous outsider who
continually provokes the audience and who will resort even to
obscene acts' (Nepoti and Cappa, p.139). Harlequin provided
Fo with a model for the subversive, derisive, mocking
character who appears in several plays. This creature is never

wholly integrated into society but never totally alienated from
it either. He has the licence granted to the Fool in
Shakespeare's *King Lear* but makes use of it not merely to
amuse the power-holder but to jeer at all he stands for. Fo's
Harlequin does not merely cavort and make fun of the
baubles the king wears round his neck but also of his right to
wear a crown at all. On another occasion, he said of
Harlequin: 'Arlecchino is someone who refuses this society
lock, stock and barrel, but not because he has another one in
mind. He is simply totally a-social. He goes straight to the
heart of things and destroys everything – honour, logic,
common sense and customs' (*Fabulazzo*, p.375). In a
conversation with Ron Jenkins, an American ex-clown turned
theatre historian, Fo went so far as to say: 'I have played
Harlequin all my life. My characters have always been along
the lines of Harlequin. Harlequin is the character who
destroys all the conventions. His personality and his sense of
morality are based on paradox. They come from nowhere and
can be transformed into anything' (ibid.).

The Maniac is the supreme, updated representation of the
Harlequin. He may not wear the traditional outfit or mask,
but has all the characteristics associated with the character: he
is cunning, scheming, disrespectful towards authority, quick-
witted, inventive, anarchic but also perceptive, incisive in his
judgements and scornful of official cant and mendacity. While
the others have professional relationships with each other and
careers they wish to advance, he exists in a dimension of his
own, owing loyalty to none. He disconcerts the police by the
nimble way he changes side, especially after the arrival of the
journalist. Initially, he seems to support the police, enabling
them to ward off some of the journalist's more probing
questions, only to change tack and encourage her in other
lines of inquiry. Earlier, he had reduced the officers to a state
of panic-stricken inertia, but then raised their spirits by the
ridiculous ruse of persuading them that they had showed
humanity to the suspect by playing with him a game of
imaginary railways. From a role as prosecuting counsel, he
has in this scene reverted to a position of pure clown,
executing the equivalent of tumbles and acrobatics.

Not much store need be set by the Maniac's supposed insanity. There is a style of madness more common on the stages of theatres than in the wards of mental hospitals, one which allows the supposedly deranged individual access to truths hidden from slower-witted individuals, or from those who have other interests to serve. The Maniac does not suffer from any neurosis, and the symptoms of his wayward behaviour, his passion for dressing up and passing himself off as other people, are invaluable both for his quest for the truth and his wish to mock. In this play, the madman is the personification of reason and guardian of public morality. He has a cause – the unveiling of police and official lies in the Pinelli case – which he prosecutes with tenacity, vigour and a grotesque humour. In his own words on *Accidental Death* to Jenkins, Fo stated: 'The fool plays the part of the judge, carrying the logic of the authorities to absurd extremes, and discovering that there are inconsistencies. For instance, if the police witnesses were telling the truth, the victim would have had to have three feet. The clown-fool uses this incongruity to establish the truth of the situation. In that way, the absurd becomes a form of logical reasoning founded on paradoxes.' Put in different terms, he does don a mask, or several successive masks, exactly like the Harlequins of old. He wears the mask of the academic psychiatrist, magistrate, bishop and member of the forensic squad. In himself, he is no one.

The Maniac was the part Fo himself played in the first productions. It has always to be borne in mind that Fo is of his essence an actor-author, not merely an actor who writes or an author who performs. He employed his own talents to make possible the endless changes of identity required by his own conception of the Maniac. This is the key role in the play.

Bertozzo

Bertozzo has the rank of *commissario,* roughly approximate to inspector in British terms. There were two inspectors involved in the actual interrogation of Pinelli, but Bertozzo's characterisation is overlaid with so much riotous humour that any identification can only be approximate. He is an amalgam of several police officers, but principally he is a creature familiar in comedy, the butt of the humour. Jokes about the *carabinieri*, one of the three police forces which operate in Italy, are as common as are jokes about flat-footed, dim-witted bobbies in Britain. Bertozzo is a comic, idiotic figure who fits that stereotype. His role is not so much to advance the satire as to arouse derisive laughter. There is something of the circus clown about him. He is first seen as the 'side-kick', or the 'straight man' in the comic routines at the start of the play, when the Maniac is brought into the police office. He is himself given no witticisms to deliver. His role is to speak deadpan, humourless lines which the Maniac will use to display his own deft wit. It is not surprising that it is Bertozzo who, having been set up by the Maniac, is the unwitting, undeserving target for the punch which the other inspector aims at him. Only once does he have a serious part to play, when he is revealed as the bomb expert who had been responsible for the suspicious act of destroying the unexploded bomb without subjecting it to forensic examination. Other than that, there is always one clown who is on the receiving end of the knockabout violence, who will have the bucket of water poured over him or the custard pie thrown in his face. In filling that role, Bertozzo will not even arouse sympathy from the audience. He is there purely as a function of comedy, as the object of satire and ridicule.

Inspector

The Inspector could be said to be the reason why the play was written. There are many incidental clues left around the play which underline that he is based, very closely, on *commissario* Luigi Calabresi. Some of these clues have, inevitably, been lost in the process of translation. In the original, on the Inspector's first entrance at the beginning of Act One, Scene Two, he is described as 'wearing a sports jacket and a polo-necked shirt'; several journalists at the time drew attention to the casual wear which Calabresi, unlike the rest of the officers, preferred. Similarly, by the time of the trial against

Pio Baldelli and *Lotta Continua,* he was noted to have the nervous twitches which Fo mentions in the play.

Even without these prompts, audiences at the time would have had no difficulty in seeing the Inspector as a lightly disguised version of Calabresi. It was Calabresi who had become the supreme hate-figure for the left, Calabresi who had been in charge of the arrests of the suspects in the earlier Fiera di Milano bombing, Calabresi whom the *Lotta Continua* newspaper had reported as being linked with the American Secret Services and with the 'Colonels'' regime in Greece, Calabresi who was identified as the 'Window-Straddler', Calabresi who was regarded as being the man chiefly responsible for the death of Pino Pinelli. On the very day of the bombing, he told a journalist of the Turin newspaper, *La Stampa,* that the 'extreme left was undoubtedly responsible'. The same day, he led the detachment of policemen who raided the anarchist circle in Via Scaldasole in Milan, and was responsible for the, seemingly chance, arrest of Pinelli. Pinelli turned up at the club after his game of cards, and was invited by Calabresi to come along for a chat. He rode to the police station on his own motorbike, following the police cars. He never left the station alive.

Since he had been the subject of many newspaper profiles and of phone-ins to radical radio stations, Calabresi's career was well known to any audience attending *Accidental Death of an Anarchist.* In 1966, he had been invited to join a CIA course in the USA. He had been in cahoots with the Republican right in America, particularly with the section of the party linked to Senator Barry Goldwater, an extreme right-wing candidate who was heavily defeated by Lyndon Johnson in the presidential race of 1964. Calabresi was believed to be fully involved in the 'strategy of tension'. Dario Fo, who satirised Calabresi mercilessly in the play and in his improvised introductions to each evening's performance, later took a gentler view of the man, considering Calabresi as another victim of the vicious campaign in which he was a pawn, not a main player.

Superintendent
Like the Inspector, the Superintendent is based closely on an
actual police officer, Marcello Guida, the head of the police in
Milan. The references in the original were quite explicit.
Guida, an older man, had been a government official under
Mussolini's Fascist regime, and in 1942 had been
commandant of a prison camp for anti-fascist activists in the
town of Ventotene in Southern Italy. These references survive
in this translation as allusions to the Superintendent's
supposed activities with mercenaries in Bosnia. The original
Guida was very insistent on the connections between the
bombings at the Fiera on 25 April and Piazza Fontana: the
left-wingers accused in both cases were later acquitted. Guida
was involved in setting up the identity parade which led to the
framing of Pietro Valpreda. He took a full part in the cover-up
after the death of Pinelli, initially denying that there were any
records of the interrogation, then changing his story. Pinelli's
widow later raised an unsuccessful action against him.

Constables
There were in fact four constables in the office at the time of
Pinelli's death, all later named in the action brought by Licia
Pinelli in connection with the death of her husband, but it
would be excessive to attempt to establish links between any
one of them and the constables Fo depicts in his work. The
two constables here are smiling, largely benign, foolish
bystanders, never fully comprehending what is going on
around them. They are in line with the incompetent village
policemen in detective stories, rather than in line with their
genuinely sinister superiors.

Journalist
With the journalist, the identification is again certain and
complete. The character of the journalist is inspired by the
campaigning writer and reporter, Camilla Cederna, who, in a
series of trenchant articles and books, doggedly investigated
the circumstances leading to the death of Pinelli.

The character has caused considerable bewilderment for directors and distress for the actresses. The problem is that while all the others make their contribution to the comedy, the journalist has a completely straight part. She is not given a line which would allow her to raise a smile, she has not a joke to deliver, nor a comic routine to participate in, except in a minor way at the end, when she is tied to the bar with the others, but by then her function is played out and she is almost anonymous. For some, she has seemed like a character from a play written by a different author, for example by Brecht in his most preachy mode. Some directors have taken this lack of comic function as a challenge to their inventiveness, and several unfortunate actresses have been required to wobble on stage in tight-fitting skirts, garish blouses, dark sunglasses, high heels and even to speak in high-pitched, squeaky voices. This approach ignores the structure and balance of this play. As Fo said of another of his works, there comes a point when laughter is no longer necessary: 'What are those laughs that we put in? We could take them out, if we wished, but they serve a purpose, to grab the attention of the audience [. . .] but the second part is more spare, without jokes, because by now the audience is inside the mechanism, by now it has accepted the approach, it is used even to suffering and can concentrate without the need of humour or laughter' (*Compagni senza censura*, p.113). The journalist contributes to the politics of the play, to creating the mood in which the questioning can be carried forward. She is not one of the farceurs.

Writing and performance history

The first problem in translating any Dario Fo script is locating a fixed, accepted text to translate. One translator, Dan Rebellato, exasperated at the sheer range of successive versions of the Fo play he was to translate, came to the wry conclusion that the work he was staging in English under Fo's name was probably being presented in that form for the very first time.

An evening attending a Fo play in Italy, especially in the militantly political period of the late sixties and early seventies, has a familiar structure. Firstly, Fo, without costume or make-up, will himself come on stage to deliver a more or less improvised prologue which will range over contemporary events in Italy and abroad but will finish with a discussion of the origins and central lines of the play itself. He has an easy but devastating and merciless wit, as the politicians, churchmen or celebrities he has lampooned have found to their cost. This part has its own importance, so while it is vital to remember that it was there, it does not normally feature in any translation. The play itself will have two acts, followed, in the late sixties and early seventies, by a debate with the audience which made up a 'third act'.

The problem for publishers, directors and translators is over the central text itself. There is never really a point when Fo's plays are rounded off and completed. They are discussed with collaborators, especially with Franca Rame, are subject to endless rewrites during the rehearsal period, can be altered in the light of audience reaction and, especially with a work like *Accidental Death*, are still liable to be modified day-by-day in response to public events. On the other hand, since his scripts are meant for performance in front of a live audience, Fo loses interest in his own work once the run is over. He is fond of pointing to the example of Shakespeare who left the chore of having his plays published to friends who put together after his death the famous folios which are the only record of his works. In Fo's case, this work is done by Franca Rame. It is she who is responsible for collating all the various versions and modifications, choosing which to retain and which to jettison, making cuts, adding stage directions and presenting the manuscript to the publisher. Even this is not necessarily the end of the process. In several cases, including *Accidental Death,* there have been quite substantial changes made for successive versions. There were three main editions of the play – the original performed in 1970 and published by Mazzotta in 1973, the 1972 revised and slightly retitled version, *Accidental Death of an Anarchist and Other Subversives,* and the version finally published by Einaudi in

1974. There were further minor changes for the version in the Complete Works published by the same company in 1988. The play has a separate history in English, of which more later.

Fo never corresponded to a romantic vision of a writer waiting for the inspiration of some interior voice. His works were written in reaction to situations occurring in society or in response to requests from activists in various fields who demanded that certain problems be made the subject of drama. *Can't Pay? Won't Pay!* was written at a time of high inflation when some housewives in Milan took matters into their own hands by taking from supermarket shelves what they required for their families. Another play, *Mum's Marijuana Is Best*, was written to meet concerns about the circulation of drugs. He himself explained the genesis of *Accidental Death of an Anarchist*:

> Where did the idea to put on a play linked to the State Massacre [the Piazza Fontana bombing] come from? In this case, as in others, we were goaded by a situation of necessity. In spring 1970, some comrades who attended our plays – worker comrades, students, progressive democrats – asked us to write a full-length play about the Milan bombs and the Pinelli killing which would treat the causes and the political consequences. The reason for this request was the terrifying lack of information surrounding the problem. Once the initial shock had passed, the press fell silent [. . .] there was an expectation that 'light would be shed', that people should wait, and not create mayhem [. . .] This was not enough. (Afterword to Einaudi edition, p.115)

Accidental Death, in other words, was conceived with the precise purpose of providing 'counter-information', of acting as counterbalance to the misinformation and lies being spread by the media of left and right. Fo was determined to widen political understanding, and was happy to create a little turmoil. In his own words, 'It is essential to cause mayhem, and with every means available, so that people who are forgetful, who read little and badly, and who read only those things which come easily to hand, should get to know how the state organised the massacre and controlled the mourning,

the anger, the distribution of medals to orphans and widows,
the funerals with policemen lining up and taking the salute.'
In the militant atmosphere of those days, pity, even for a man
who met his death in custody, was not a consideration.

> There should be no tears shed over the death of a comrade.
> Anyone who does so risks putting up with everything. Since it was
> a comrade who died at our side, we must make every effort to
> grasp the political meaning of his death. There is no call for
> emotional display, since an emotional outpouring carries the risk
> of 'digesting' the play and being left with the joy of a beautifully
> clear conscience. (Introduction to Mazzotta edition, p.139)

Fo collected available material assiduously. He made use of
the two official inquiries, the first conducted by Judge Caizzi
in May 1970 and the second by Judge Amati in July of the
same year. Both reports are quoted, sometimes verbatim, as
dialogue in the play. Friendly journalists and lawyers
provided information contained in articles their papers would
not publish. He received help from Camilla Cederna, the
model for the journalist in the play, and from Guido Savelli,
author of *La strage di stato: contro-inchiesta* (The State
Massacre: Counter-Inquiry). The phrase 'state massacre', an
equivalent of other expressions like 'state funeral', entered the
language to designate the responsibilities of organs of the
state for the bombing and the cover-up.

Fo always writes at top speed, so the first version of the
script was ready by mid-1970. His company was La Comune,
which had by then acquired its own venue, the Capannone in
Milan. Since it was a co-operative, the agreement of the
members was required, so Fo read his script to the group and
was granted approval. It is worth noting that this approval
was not automatic. A play on the topic of education written
by another well-respected playwright, Vittorio Franceschi,
was read on the same occasion but not approved since it was
believed to lack the necessary 'class sense'. The premiere of
Accidental Death of an Anarchist took place on 10 December
1970. At the same time, the trial of Pio Baldelli was under
way across the city. Baldelli was editor of the left-wing daily,
Lotta Continua, who had been sued for criminal libel by

Inspector Calabresi for alleging that he was responsible for Pinelli's death. The script of the play was altered continually to incorporate revelations made at the trial. Fo later wrote that when he staged *Accidental Death of an Anarchist,* he did not have the advantage of having 'great actors' alongside him. 'They were all right, but the play worked very well anyway.' This assessment of the quality of his actors, while grudging, may be true, but he plainly made enormous demands of them. His explanation of the success of the performance was that 'they were all good "straight-men", and for a "straight-man" to work, he has to be cold, almost detached [. . .] It does not matter whether he possesses great charisma or charm. What counts is that he keeps the tempo and lets the lead actor take over' (*Dialogo provocatorio,* p.41).

However, while *Accidental Death of an Anarchist* was conceived as a political play, its success in Italy at the time was due in no small measure, and its international success thereafter was due almost entirely, to its comic brio and inventiveness. As a farce, with its rhythms, interlocking mechanism of plot and hilarious dialogue, the play was perfectly conceived and constructed. Fo has always been insistent that the twin elements of farce and political engagement go hand in hand and be properly balanced in any production. As he wrote in 1990, twenty years after his own first production:

Let us take *Accidental Death of an Anarchist,* viewed, indeed catalogued, as a classic example of explicitly political theatre. Yes, there is the inquest conducted on an incident which occurred in the police station – the famous drop of the anarchist from the window. Perhaps a crime, a state crime, a murder they clumsily tried to pass off as suicide. But the key to the plot is the fact that it is located in an entertaining situation. To unleash the comedy and satire, the character of a madman was chosen, a maniac with a passion for disguise who, through the logic of wild paradox, attempts to unhinge the logic of sane people. So as it happens the real madmen turn out to be the 'normal' folk. Mad and criminal into the bargain! This game of the grotesque, of paradox, of madness is one which could very well stand on its own, without the support of the political element. (Ibid., p.149)

This is not to say that Fo has any sympathy with efforts of directors to separate the two elements of madcap farce and political engagement. In the same passage, he denounced with bitter irony 'some directors (may God break them on the wheel!), who in a drive to create pure entertainment have removed all realistic reference to the conflict, have overdone the comedy and ended up with a clown show. What they produced is nothing more than a kind of surreal farce where there is no shortage of belly laughs but where people leave the theatre without any sense of indignation or any ideas which might cause disturbance.'

It was no part of Fo's scheme to be unduly subtle in his approach or intentions. Ambiguity was not a quality he admired. In the discussions which followed *Accidental Death of an Anarchist,* he invited, and received, dissent, but argued vigorously in defence of his own beliefs and techniques. He cared passionately about both the political debate in his theatre and about the theatrical techniques employed. He delightedly quoted the Chinese leader, Mao Tse-tung, to the effect that someone who uses the theatre purely as propaganda does a disservice both to theatre and to politics. 'The theatre is a guarantor of thoughts, ideas, knowledge,' he told one audience, but added, 'it is a deforming lens, a kind of bastard mirror which makes you bigger, gives you a grotesque vision of yourself and lets you read things which you would never manage to read with your ordinary eyes' (*Compagni senza censura*, p.216). In theatrical terms, Fo set out to make his point by focused humour, irony, satire and the use of the grotesque.

The choice of the Maniac as central character in a play on the death of a comrade perplexed many of his supporters. The audience was compelled to view through the eyes of the Maniac the action onstage and the events offstage on which the plot was based. It was he who was responsible for holding up the comic distorting lens, or for offering images in the distorting mirror of the grotesque which, paradoxically, made them more true. Fo slapped down a questioner who doubted whether it was appropriate to treat a tragic subject in such a light-hearted way.

It must always be clear that the one who provides the viewpoint is the Maniac. And how can I go about making it clear at every moment that it is always the Maniac who is speaking, that it is the Maniac who plays the Judge-character, that it is the Maniac who at every moment plays the police captain, the Maniac who plays the bishop? I need his outrageous humour and presence. Because I must have people aware – this is the technique of theatre – that the things that he says are tremendously dramatic but the means, the development, the character are completely abstract, crazy, incongruous and, above all, improbable [. . .] It is banal to insist that serious things have to be said in a serious way [. . .] No, I prefer to have something comic narrated in a serious way, and a dramatic statement made through the grotesque. A bit more imagination, a bit more inventiveness. (Ibid., p.190)

In the first edition, the action appeared to have been switched to America. An anarchist named Salsedo had died in circumstances similar to those in which Pinelli met his end, by falling from the fourteenth floor of the police station. I have never been able to ascertain whether there was such a man, but the truth or otherwise of the Salsedo ruse scarcely matters. However, in an intricate game of double-bluff, Fo announces a scheme to make matters more immediate for his Italian audience. Although he is dealing with 'something which really did occur in America in 1921', he explains:

So as to update and make the events more dramatic, we have taken the liberty of making use of one of those stratagems which are commonly employed in theatre, that is, we have brought the entire story forward to our own days, and instead of New York we have set it in an Italian city chosen at random . . . let us say Milan. Logically and in order to avoid anachronisms, we have been obliged to call the sheriffs *commissari* and the inspectors *questori*. (Ibid., p.141)

The logic is very much tongue-in-cheek, and Fo made jokes about the imaginary American setting to his audience, deliberately confusing Bergamo and San Francisco. No one was expected to be fooled, all the more so since the Mazzotta edition was illustrated with line drawings by Fo which

showed the impossibility of a still-alive man falling at the
angle at which Pinelli would have needed to fall to land where
he did. In the prologue to the first production, Fo used these
drawings in slides which he showed to the audience.

The ending underwent changes as deep as the opening.
Initially, the ending was in line with the one used in the
present English-language edition. The magistrate who enters
at the end is attacked by the policemen who have slipped their
handcuffs, but who then discover to their dismay that they
are assaulting the 'real' magistrate whose task is to conduct
the 'real' inquiry. Fo explained this ending:

> What happened was there was darkness, a shout was heard and a
> bomb went off somewhere. Then the lights went on and the
> Maniac was no longer there. The journalist ran over to look out
> the window – because she had undone the lock, she had got free –
> and she realised that the Maniac had fallen. Who had touched
> him, who had thrown him out? There is a doubt. The doubt arises
> from the fact that one of the policemen absent-mindedly, while
> saying goodbye to the journalist, pulls his hand out of the
> handcuffs without any problem, and everyone notices that he is
> free. Doubt: it is not self-destruction. But then another judge
> comes in, who is exactly the same as the previous one, as the
> Maniac, a bit fatter, with a double chin, more full of himself,
> speaking a little differently, but who must be the spitting image of
> the other one. And he says – let us get on with the inquiry. What
> in the last analysis did this ending say? It said that if one day there
> were to be an inquiry, and a judge really were to come, nothing
> would change. Because it is not by holding inquiries that you
> change the system. That is to say that it is not the fact that there
> was no inquiry in Italy on the Pinelli case that shows that our
> social democracy stinks. No! It would stink a bit less, but it would
> still stink. (Ibid., pp.208–9)

In later versions, the Maniac gets hold of the bomb, forces
Bertozzo to give up his gun and handcuffs him to the rail
along with the others. He announces that he has recorded the
entire conversation, that he will dispatch the recording to the
newspapers and unleash a scandal. He has, of course, little
faith in the power of scandals to bring about fundamental

change, but at least the scandal will put the Italians on the
same level as the Americans, the British and other social
democracies. The Italian people will be able to exclaim 'we
are up to the necks in shit, which is why we walk with our
heads held high'. With these elegant words, he saunters
offstage.

English-language versions
There are specific problems, endlessly discussed, in translating
drama, involving the need to release an energy which may be
conveyed by silence as much as by speech, to find devices to
communicate stage business, to ensure that dialogue is
speakable as well as faithful to the original, to accommodate
performance traditions as well as accuracy, to transpose
humour. There are two specific difficulties in the case of Fo:
finding a means of communicating to a non-Italian audience
the information on political events Fo was able to take for
granted with his own audiences, and finding a way of
combining his own brand of humour with the political
fire. The end product must be stimulating and entertaining
for an audience whose cultural expectations are different.

To make matters more complex, Fo's manner of
playwriting assumes that the distance between the page and
the stage is very small. It is significant that he once quoted
with approval a view expressed by Bertolt Brecht on
Shakespeare. 'A pity he [Shakespeare] reads so beautifully. It
is his only defect, but a great one.' Fo adds his own comment:
'And Brecht was right. However paradoxical it may seem, a
genuine work of theatre should not at all appear a pleasure
when read: its worth should become apparent only on the
stage' (*Tricks of the Trade*, p.183). *Accidental Death* may be,
to some extent, an exception but Fo's plays are rarely funny
when read. They require that extra element which is provided
by live performance, particularly when the performer is Fo
himself.

His plays, when written, were hard-hitting satire, and
many translators and directors have wondered whether that
directness of aim can be retained by straight translation, or

whether Fo is best served by some form of adaptation. The fact, as a glance at the bibliography of works by Fo in English will show, is that more frequently than with any other foreign-language author he has been deemed to require the intervention of an adapter. Of course, no translation is ever totally 'literal' in any meaningful sense of the word, but it is still vital to make the distinction between translation and adaptation. A translation indicates a process where the transposition between cultures is purely linguistic, and where the translator respects the setting, the period, the characterisation and the historical particularities chosen by the author in his/her writing. An adaptation involves a wider switch, where the adapter, who in Britain is likely to be different from the translator, makes alterations designed to update, to change setting, to alter the topic of any discussion or satire, to modify character or in some other way to domesticate and make more familiar what is foreign and strange.

The first production of *Accidental Death* in Britain was very much an adaptation, and one which Dario Fo himself strenuously objected to. *Can't Pay? Won't Pay!*, itself an adaptation by Robert Walker, was an unexpected success in the West End in 1981, and led to demand for more Fo, satisfied by the production of *Accidental Death* by the Belt and Braces company. The translation was done by Gillian Hanna, but the main spirit was Gavin Richards, who did the adaptation and played the main role. The production was enormously successful, and this became the standard form of the play in Britain for many years. However, the distances between the play Fo wrote and the version mounted on the British stage were considerable, and these were heightened when the company broadcast the play on Channel Four in 1983 to the point that all contact between Fo and the work now masquerading as his was lost.

The Richards version, perhaps unintentionally, reduced the political impact of the play. In his view, the script written by Fo could be manipulated and reordered at will, provided the resultant production was viable in itself. The policemen in their work were simple boobies, London's answer to the

Keystone Cops of the silent cinema. They were capable of acts of brutality, but this violence was the behaviour of unintelligent thugs, not the work of people acting in accord with some plan, elements of which were beyond their ken. Richards allowed the play to move from slapstick to propaganda, without any attempt to co-ordinate the two or to see them as part of the one vision of popular theatre. The rationale for the disguise of the Maniac as the bishop evidently escaped him, so he cut it out altogether. There was more logic to his decision to change the references in the Maniac's speech on scandals, so that instead of the Italian allusions, he introduced talk of Sir Anthony Blunt, a Buckingham Palace art specialist who had been a Soviet spy, and Blair Peach, a protester who had been killed in a demonstration in London. It was curious that in productions in Britain years later, these references were not themselves updated. Richards even introduced slighting remarks on Fo into the text:

Inspector   This is an unheard of distortion of the author's meaning!
Maniac   He'll get his royalties. Who's moaning?
Inspector   Get back to the script!
Superintendent   This is an insult to Dario Fo.
Journalist   Good. I've got a bone to pick with him. Why is there only one woman's part in his blasted play?
Maniac   The author's sexist?
Journalist   He's pre-historic!

The climax to the English adaptation was a completely new double ending. In this version, the journalist runs off with the recording, leaving the policemen tied up and the bomb ticking. The bomb goes off, and the Maniac, who acts here as a chorus, comments to the audience, 'Now that's what I would call a happy ending.' However, he then calls the journalist back for the alternative ending where, moved by compassion, she releases them only to find herself double-crossed when they seize her, handcuff her to the bar and wander off leaving her to listen to the ticking of the bomb. The Maniac then issues a direct challenge to the audience:

'Oh *Dio!* Whichever way it goes, you've got to decide.
Goodnight!'

Dario Fo was present at the first night, and had to be
restrained at the interval. His belief – or the publishable part
of it – was that Richards had failed to appreciate the element
of tragedy in the play, and had played it all for laughs. It is,
however, possible to sympathise with Fo's dismay and still
appreciate the qualities of the production, especially since
Richards never claimed to be presenting the British public
with a faithful translation. His adaptation involved a switch
of theatrical culture, from an Italian *commedia dell'arte* style
to a messier style based on British music hall. It was not Fo
and was more vacuous than the original, but it had a fire, a
drive and a comic force of its own, and these may have helped
compensate for its other inadequacies.

When in 1990 the Royal National Theatre in London
decided to incorporate the play, by now a 'modern classic',
into their touring repertoire, they commissioned a new
translation, which was then adapted by the director, Tim
Supple, and the lead actor, Alan Cumming. They consulted
Fo himself, and were intent on producing a version which was
in line with his original script. As they wrote:

> From the outset, we knew that a revival of *Accidental Death of an
> Anarchist* must grow directly from Fo's original text. Even in
> original translation, we were aware of an uncomplicated satire –
> as real and as brutally human as those who interrogated Pinelli –
> that we had not recognised in other English adaptations. We
> understood how, as Fo put it, tragedy had been turned into farce:
> the farce of power. (Methuen edition, 1991, p.xxiii)

In view of this, they promised in words carried in the
programme, but curiously omitted from the book, that 'all
temptation to impose verbal wit, cartoon characters and
satisfying structure were to be resisted: they belong to a
different tradition and spirit from Fo's'. This did not mean
reproducing Fo's play as he had written it. They chose an
imprecise setting, half-Italy and half-England, had one of the
policemen strut about pantomime-style between acts but
conveyed on stage a sense of their menace, and used the play

as a vehicle to slam injustices perpetrated in Britain. They wrote, 'We have our own farces of power: two of which began in the hunt for the Guildford and Birmingham bombings 16 years ago, and are still being played out.' From these disparate elements, they hoped to offer a 'comic dialogue with our audiences to be made up of many farces'. They also hoped to 'show Italy through a British filter and so, we hope, to see both clearly'.

Subsequently Ed Emery produced a third version which was more faithful to Fo's original. In his explanation of his operation, he said that he had maintained 'the original references', but he trusted that companies would use their imagination and 'adapt the political and cultural references to suit their own requirements'. The present translation by Simon Nye has made its own choice of references, and has chosen to set the play unambiguously in Britain.

The play never found the favour in North America which it did in Britain, due, it would appear, to the poor quality of the adaptations and the productions. In all cases, companies have sought to emphasise the comedy at the expense of the politics, and in one New York production, even introduced songs, to the dismay of Fo who was in the audience. Fo made them remove them, and felt his work was the better for this decision. He himself, mournfully, quoted a review in the *New York Times*, in which the critic wrote that 'in this production, there are two deaths. The first and most obvious is that of the script' (*Dialogo provocatorio*, p.150). This is not a comment which this play deserves, nor one which will be made of the present witty and lively translation.

Further Reading

Plays by Dario Fo and Franca Rame in Italian

The theatrical works of Dario Fo and Franca Rame have gone
through various editions with various publishers. There is a
collected edition, edited by Rame, published by Einaudi,
which runs so far to thirteen volumes. The early works are
credited to Fo alone, while the later volumes are catalogued
as the work of both Dario Fo and Franca Rame. A few of the
pieces from the early eighties onwards were written by Rame
alone, some were collaborative works but the majority were
written by Fo.

Plays by Fo in English

1) Anthologies. There are two volumes of selected plays, by
different translators:

Plays: One (contains *Mistero Buffo, Accidental Death of an
    Anarchist, Trumpets and Raspberries, The Virtuous
    Burglar, One Was Nude and One Wore Tails*), London,
    Methuen, 1992
Plays: Two (contains *Can't Pay? Won't Pay!, Elizabeth, The
    Open Couple, An Ordinary Day*), London, Methuen, 1994

2) *Accidental Death of an Anarchist*. The present translation
is the fourth to appear in the UK. The others are:

Accidental Death of an Anarchist, trans. Gillian Hanna,
    adapted by Gavin Richards, London, Pluto Press, 1980;
    Methuen, 1987
Accidental Death of an Anarchist, adapted by Alan Cumming
    and Tim Supple, London, Methuen, 1991

Accidental Death of an Anarchist, trans. Ed Emery, in *Plays: One*, London, Methuen, 1992

3) Other plays:

Coming Home, trans. Ed Emery, London, Theatretexts, 1984
The Mother, trans. Ed Emery, London, Theatretexts, 1984
The Rape, trans. Ed Emery, London, Theatretexts, 1984
The Tale of a Tiger, trans. Ed Emery, London, Theatretexts, 1984
Archangels Don't Play Pinball, trans. R.C. McAvoy and Anna-Maria Giugni, London, Methuen, 1986
The Tale of a Tiger, trans. Ron Jenkins, *Theater,* vol. 21, winter 1990
A Woman Alone & Other Plays, trans. Ed Emery, Gillian Hanna, Christopher Cairns, London, Methuen, 1991
The Pope and the Witch, trans. Ed Emery, adapted by Andy de la Tour, London, Methuen, 1992
Abducting Diana, trans. Rupert Lowe, adapted by Stephen Stenning, London, Oberon, 1994
The Devil in Drag, trans. Ed Emery, in *New Connections 99,* London, Faber and Faber, 1999

Works by Fo referred to in the text

Compagni senza censura (2 vols), Milan, Mazzotta, 1970 and 1973
Il teatro politico di Dario Fo, Milan, Mazzotta, 1977
Dialogo provocatorio sul comico, il tragico, la follia e la ragione (conversation with Luigi Allegri), Bari, Laterza, 1990
Totò: manuale dell'attore comico, Turin, Aleph, 1990; 2nd ed., Florence, Vallecchi, 1995
Fabulazzo (collection of occasional articles), ed. Lorenzo Ruggiero and Walter Valeri, Milan, Kaos, 1991
Vladimir Majakovskij: Messaggi ai posteri selezionati e condivisi da Dario Fo (selection of writings by Mayakovsky, with connecting commentary by Fo), Rome, Editori Riuniti, 1999

Tricks of the Trade, trans. Joseph Farrell, London, Methuen, 1987

Works on Fo

1) *Biographical*

Behan, Tom, *Dario Fo: Revolutionary Theatre*, London, Pluto Press, 2000
Farrell, Joseph, *Dario Fo & Franca Rame: Harlequins of the Revolution*, London, Methuen, 2001
Fo, Dario, *My First Seven Years (plus a few more)*, trans. Joseph Farrell, London, Methuen, 2005

2) *Critical approaches*

General works:

Ballerini, Luigi and Risso, Giuseppe, *Dario Fo Explains: An Interview*, in *Drama Review*, vol. 22, no. 1, March 1978, pp. 34–48
Cappa, Marina, and Nepoti, Roberto, *Dario Fo*, Rome, Gremese, 1982
Cowan, Suzanne, 'The Throw-away Theatre of Dario Fo', in *Drama Review*, no. 2, 1975, pp. 103–13
Emery, Ed (ed.), *Dario Fo and Franca Rame: Theatre Workshops at Riverside Studios, London* (includes, scripts, interviews and workshop proceedings), London, Red Notes, 1983
Emery, Ed (ed.), *Dario Fo and Franca Rame* (proceedings of international conference on Fo and Rame), London, Red Notes, 2002
Farrell, Joseph and Scuderi, Antonio (eds), *Dario Fo: Stage, Text, and Tradition*, Carbondale and Edwardsville, Southern Illinois University Press, 2000
Hirst, David, *Dario Fo and Franca Rame*, London, Macmillan, 1989

Jenkins, Ron, *Dario Fo & Franca Rame: Artful Laughter*,
New York, Aperture, 2001

Jenkins, Ron, 'Clowns and Popes in Italy', in *Subversive
Laughter*, New York, Free Press, 1994, pp. 107–332

Mitchell, Tony, *Dario Fo: People's Court Jester*, London,
Methuen (2nd ed.), 1999

Mitchell, Tony, *File on Dario Fo*, London, Methuen, 1989

Mitchell, Tony, 'Dario Fo: The Histrionics of Class Struggle',
in *Gambit*, vol.9, no.36, 1980, pp. 55–60

Pertile, Lino, 'Dario Fo', in *Writers and Society in
Contemporary Italy*, ed. Michael Caesar and Peter
Hainsworth, Oxford, Oxford University Press, 1984, pp.
167–90

Scuderi, Antonio, *Dario Fo and Popular Performance*,
Ottawa, Legas, 1998

Sogliuzzo, A. Richard, 'Puppets for a Proletarian Revolution',
in *Drama Review*, no. 3, 1972, pp. 72–7

Valeri, Walter (ed.), *Franca Rame: A Woman on Stage,* West
Lafayette, Bordighera, 1999

Articles or chapters on *Accidental Death of an Anarchist:*

Bentley, Eric, 'Was This Death Accidental?', in *Theater*,
vol.16, no.2, p.66

Dahl, Mary Karen, 'State Terror and Dramatic Counter-
measures', in John Orr and Klaic Dragan, *Terrorism and
Modern Drama*, Edinburgh, Edinburgh University Press,
1990, pp. 109–21

Fitzpatrick, Tim, and Sawczak, Ksenia, 'Accidental Death of
the Translator: The Difficult Case of Dario Fo', in *About
Performance*, Centre for Performance Studies, University of
Sydney, 1995, pp.15–33

Lorch, Jennifer (ed.), *Morte accidentale di un anarchico* (text
in Italian, intro. and notes in English), Manchester,
Manchester University Press, 1997

Lorch, Jennifer, '*Morte accidentale* in English', in *Dario Fo:
Stage, Text, and Tradition,* op.cit.

Historical background to *Accidental Death of an Anarchist*

Cederna, Camilla, *Pinelli, una finestra sulla strage*, Milan, Feltrinelli, 1971

Ginsborg, Paul, *A History of Contemporary Italy, Society and Politics 1943–1988*, London, Penguin, 1990

Gundle, Stephen and Parker, Stephen (eds), *The New Italian Republic*, London, Routledge, 1996

Jones, Tobias, *The Dark Heart of Italy*, London, Faber, 2003

Lumley, Robert, *States of Emergency: Culture of Revolt in Italy from 1968–1978*, London, Verso, 1990

Lumley, Robert, *Italian Journalism* (an anthology of writings in Italian containing a useful section on Piazza Fontana), Manchester, Manchester University Press, 1996

Mack Smith, Denis, *Modern Italy: A Political History*, New Haven and London, Yale University Press, 1997

Savelli, Guido (ed.), *La strage di stato: contro-inchiesta*, Rome, Newton Compton, 1970

Willan, Philip, *Puppetmasters: The Political Use of Terrorism in Italy*, London, Constable, 1991

Accidental Death of an Anarchist

translated by Simon Nye

...slation of *Accidental Death of an Anarchist* was first ...formed at the Donmar Warehouse, London, on 20 February 2003. The cast was as follows:

Bertozzo	Desmond Barrit
Maniac	Rhys Ifans
Constable/s	Cornelius Booth
Inspector	Paul Ritter
Superintendent	Adrian Scarborough
Journalist	Emma Amos

Director Robert Delamere
Designer Simon Higlett
Lighting Designer Paul Pyant
Sound Designer Paul Arditti

Act One

Scene One

A nondescript room at central police headquarters, somewhere in England. A desk, a cupboard, a few chairs, computer, telephone, window and two doors. The time is now.

A man's face appears at the window. We are clearly high up, on the third floor. He looks inside, then tests the window, which opens. He pulls himself inside, carrying a large bag. He stands there, very much at ease: the **Maniac**.

The door opens and **Inspector Bertozzo** *comes in, followed by a uniformed* **Constable**. *The three men freeze as they notice each other.* **Bertozzo** *and the* **Maniac** *know each other.*

Bertozzo   What are you doing here?

Maniac   I'm here to – no, you work it out, I'm a tax-payer. Potentially.

Bertozzo *nods to the* **Constable**, *who grabs the* **Maniac** *with some force.*

Bertozzo   Get his file.

The **Constable** *indicates that his hands are full.* **Bertozzo** *sighs heavily and walks the few feet to his desk, where the* **Maniac**'s *file is in a pile of others.* **Bertozzo** *studies the file.*

Bertozzo   Ah good, there's a charge outstanding against you: impersonation. Again. Let's look at your previous . . . Surgeon, twice. Captain in the Gurkhas. Bishop, three times. Naval engineer. You've been arrested a total of . . . two and three is five . . . one, three, two . . . eleven times. So this is the twelfth little performance.

Maniac   Yes, but I would point out, Inspector Bertozzo, that I've never been found guilty. My nose is clean.

Bertozzo   Yeah, I don't know what stories you came up with to manage that, but this time – *fact* – I'm going to dirty your nose.

Maniac   I know what you're saying: I'm the same with lovely fresh snow, I can't walk past it without wanting to piss on it.

Bertozzo   Yeah, be funny. And now you've attempted to pass yourself off as a 'Professor of psychiatry and former lecturer at the University of Des Moines'. You realise that constitutes fraud and you're looking at a prison sentence?

Maniac   Yes, if I were a sane person. But I am mad. I have a certificate. It's all there in my medical records. I've been admitted sixteen times with what's called 'acting mania'. It's more of a hobby, really – playing other people. I'll do anybody! But the thing is I'm a huge fan of the Theatre of Life, so my fellow actors have to be real people . . . who don't know they're acting. Which is just as well because I'm a bit short of funds, so I can't pay them. I asked the Arts Council for a grant but I don't know anyone who's anyone, you see, so . . .

Bertozzo   So you con these so-called fellow actors.

Maniac   I have never exploited anyone in my life.

Bertozzo (*glances in file*)   As a phoney psychiatrist you charged two hundred pounds per consultation.

Constable (*standing behind the* **Maniac**)   Fuck me.

Maniac   That is the standard rate for any self-respecting psychiatrist who's studied for as many years as I have.

Bertozzo   Uh huh, what form did this studying take?

Maniac   Twenty years spent in sixteen different mental institutions studying thousands of lunatics like myself, day in day out. And at night too. Because, unlike your bog-standard psychiatrist, I've always slept with my patients – three of us top to tail because you can't get the beds, you see. Anyway, judge me by my record – in this case my startling but accurate diagnosis of a posh boy's schizophrenia, his treatment tragically curtailed by my arrest.

Bertozzo   Two hundred quid's pretty startling, too.

Maniac   Well, funnily enough, it's important that they pay a lot of money.

Bertozzo   That's part of the therapy, is it?

Maniac   Oh yes. If I hadn't stung him for two hundred do you think that poor bastard's family would have been satisfied? If I'd asked for fifty quid they'd have thought: 'Oh, he can't be much good, maybe he isn't a real professor, he must have just qualified.' *This* way, after they'd recovered from the fee, you could see them thinking: 'Well, he must be up there with Professor Anthony Clare,' and they skipped off happily. 'Thank you, Professor.' Lots of weeping.

Bertozzo   You're not bad at the old chatting, then.

Maniac   I'm not making this up. Even Freud says: 'Big fee, Quick recover-ee . . .' And doctor and patient are both literally laughing.

Bertozzo   I believe you. Let's take a look at your business card. Ooh, look: Professor Anthony Rabbi. Psychiatrist. Formerly lecturer at the University of Des Moines. Get out of that!

Maniac   First of all, I do lecture – I teach drawing at evening classes down the road at the Church of the Sacred Redeemer.

Bertozzo   Congratulations. But it says here 'Psychiatrist'.

Maniac   Very good, but after the full stop. Are you familiar with syntax and punctuation? Look closely: Professor Anthony Rabbi. Full stop. Then Psychiatrist with a capital P. You're not impersonating anyone if you say, 'I'm a bit of a psychiatrist'. We all say, 'Hey, I'm a bit of a psychologist, me'. Or a botanist. Or a bigamist. Are you *au fait* with our language and grammar? You are. Well you'll know then that 'archaeologist' doesn't mean 'has academic qualifications in archaeology' any more than 'vegetarian' means 'has academic qualifications in vegetables'.

Bertozzo   All right, but what about 'Formerly lecturer at the University of Des Moines'?

Maniac   I'm sorry but now *you're* guilty of fraud. You said you knew the language and now it's obvious you can't even read properly.

Bertozzo   What am I supposed to have got wrong?

Maniac   Didn't you see the comma after 'formerly'?

Bertozzo   Um, yeah, okay, there's a comma. I didn't think it was important.

Maniac   You 'didn't think it was important'. And because you 'didn't think it was important' an innocent man goes to prison.

Bertozzo   You really are mental, aren't you? What is the purpose of the comma?

Maniac   None whatsoever, if you're an ignorant bastard. What qualifications have you got? How did you ever get promoted? (**Bertozzo** *tries to interrupt.*) Let me finish! The comma is crucial. If there's a comma after 'formerly', the meaning of the whole sentence changes. The comma makes you take a breath, a momentary hiatus, because: 'a comma always indicates modified intentionality' . . .

So this is how it reads: 'Formerly' – a little sneer works well here, you might even throw in an ironic little whinny. So: 'Formerly,' (*He grimaces and does a snigger.*) 'lecturer at the University,' – another comma – 'of Des Moines.' As if to say: Come on, you tosspot. Who are you trying to kid!? Only a bird-witted ponce would fall for that.

Bertozzo   Are you saying I'm a bird-witted ponce?

Maniac   No, you're just a bit rubbish at grammar.
I can give you some lessons, if you like. Nothing too pricey.
Let's start right away – what are the pronouns of time and
place – ?

Bertozzo   Stop taking the piss! I've worked you out: you
really do have this acting mania, so you're acting mad but in
fact you're saner than I am.

Maniac   Why you cheeky. . . Well, there's no doubt that
being a policeman can do your head in. Let me look at your
eyes.

He pulls down **Bertozzo**'s *eyelid with his thumb.*

Bertozzo   Okay, stop that, we've got your statement to
get through.

Maniac   I'll type, if you like. I'm a qualified typist. Forty-
five words a minute.

Bertozzo   Shut up or I'll put the cuffs on you.

Maniac   You're not allowed. Straitjacket or nothing.
Handcuffing a mad person contravenes Article 122 of the
penal code: 'Any public official applying non-medical or
non-psychiatric restraining devices to a mentally disturbed
person shall be committing a crime punishable by five to
fifteen years in prison with loss of pension rights and rank.'

Bertozzo   So you know a bit about the law too.

Maniac   The law? I know everything there is to know.
I've been studying it for twenty years.

Bertozzo   How old are you – three hundred? Where did
you study law?

Maniac   In the lunatic asylum. *Fantastic* place to study.
There was a paranoid clerk of the court in there who gave
me lessons. Genius. He taught me everything – international
law, jurisprudence, human rights legislation, common law,
ecclesiastical law, the offside law, *LA Law*, mother-in-law –
everything. Test me.

Bertozzo   I haven't got time. Your CV here doesn't mention 'lawyer'.

Maniac   Oh, I could never be a lawyer. I don't like defending, that's all a bit passive. I like judging, sentencing, going after people. I'm like your good self, Inspector. Call me Tony.

Bertozzo   Listen, nutcase . . . go easy on the piss-taking.

Maniac   What did I say!?

Bertozzo   I'm surprised you haven't had a bash at a judge.

Maniac   Sadly the chance has never arisen. I would love to, though – it's got to be the best job in the world. Mainly because they never retire. At an age when your average working man's on the scrapheap – fifty-five, sixty – because he's slowing down a bit . . . that's when a judge's career really takes off. Worker on a production line's past it at fifty – trouble keeping up, making the odd slip-up, out you go! Your miner's got silicosis by the time he's forty-five – off he trots, sacked, before he's entitled to a pension. Bank clerk, same thing, at a certain age you start to muddle up accounts, you can't remember clients' names, interest rates, you can't tell an ISA from a frigging Tessa. Go home, you're all old and gaga. Whereas for a judge, it's the opposite: the older and more gaga – I'm sorry, 'delightfully eccentric' – they get, the more they're promoted. There they are, little old blokes like ancient puppets, weighed down with sashes and ermine-trimmed capes and wacky wigs. Two pairs of glasses on a chain round their neck so they can't sit on them. And these people have the power to destroy someone's life or save it. They dole out life sentences the way you and I muse about the weather. 'Fifty years for you . . . thirty for you. I'm only going to give you twenty because I rather like you.'

Yep, I'd love to play a judge just once in my life. High Court judge, ahh: 'Your Honour, do come in. Silence in court. Oh, look, someone's lost their marbles. Are they yours?' 'No, they can't be, I lost mine years ago.'

Bertozzo You're doing my head in. Sit down there and shut up.

He pushes him towards the chair.

Maniac (*reacting hysterically*) Oi – get your hands off me or I'll bite!

Bertozzo What are you talking about?

Maniac I'll bite you! First your neck then your arse. Nyum! And under Article 122 subsection B you are so stuffed: Provocation and violence vis-à-vis a person of diminished responsibility. Six to nine years with loss of pension.

Bertozzo Sit down or I'll really lose it. (*To the* **Constable**.) What are you doing there like a zombie? Make him sit down.

Constable But . . . he bites, sir.

Maniac Yes, I bloody do. Grrrr, grrr. And I should probably warn you that I have rabies. Got it from a dog. Big rabid bastard bit half my backside off. He died but I got better. Though I am still contagious: magggrrrrr! Uhuooooh!

Bertozzo A nutter with rabies – cheers. Right, are you going to let me take a statement or not? Come on, good boy. Then I'll let you go. Have we got a deal?

Maniac No, don't throw me out, Inspector. I love it here with you, among policemen. I feel safe. It's so dangerous out there on the street – nasty people, cars everywhere, horns parping, brakes squealing. Everyone's on strike! And there's buses and tube trains with vicious doors going snaaaap . . . Let me stay here with you. I'll help you get your suspects to talk. Get those lefties blabbing. I know how to make nitroglycerine suppositories!

Bertozzo   That's enough! You're annoying me now.

Maniac   Inspector, let me stay, or I'll throw myself out of the window. What floor are we on? The third? Yeah, that should do it. And when I'm down there on the pavement – dying, basically – smashed and groaning – I'm not one to die easily, so I'll do a fair amount of groaning – journalists will arrive and I'll tell them – groan, groan, groan – how you threw me down here. Okay, let's do it!

Bertozzo   Stop, please. (*To the* **Constable**.) Lock the window!

The **Constable** *does so*.

Maniac   Fine, I'll throw myself down the stairs.

He heads for the door.

Bertozzo   For God's sake! I've really had enough now. Sit down. (*He forces him down into the chair. To the* **Constable**.) You, lock the door. Take the key . . .

Maniac   . . . and throw it out the window.

The **Constable** *heads mindlessly for the window.*

Bertozzo   Yes, throw it – NO, put it in the drawer. Lock the drawer. Take the key . . .

The **Constable**, *on autopilot, does what he says.*

Maniac   Put it in your mouth and swallow it.

Bertozzo   No, no, bloody NO. Nobody gives me the run-around. (*To the* **Constable**.) Give me the key. (*He opens the door and viciously tries to push the* **Maniac** *out.*) Out. Go away. Throw yourself down the stairs if you want to. Go on – leave, before I go mad.

Maniac   No, you can't go mad, that's my thing! Don't push. Come on, why are you chucking me out? It's not my stop.

Bertozzo   Out! (*He shuts the* **Maniac** *outside the door.*) At last.

Constable   Just to remind you, Inspector, we have a meeting with Forensics . . . five minutes ago.

Bertozzo (*looks at watch*)   Bugger. That freak's mucked up my routine. Let's go.

They exit stage left. The **Maniac** *reappears stage right, the door he just left through.*

Maniac   Anybody the-ere? Inspector? Stay calm, I've just come to get my paperwork . . . Don't be cross, come on. Let's be friends again . . . Oh, nobody here. I'll just take it myself, then. My medical records. Visiting card. Charge sheet . . . Let's just tear that up. Put that behind us, thank you. (*Picks up more pieces of paper.*) Somebody else been a naughty boy? (*Reads.*) 'Embezzlement with insulting behaviour . . .' Interesting offence. Yeah, as if. Go on, lad, off you go. (*He throws the charge sheets out of the window.*) All of you can go free. (*He stops as he notices one sheet in particular.*) Ooh no, not you, you're scum. Stay here – you're going down.

He puts that charge sheet on the table where it can be seen, then goes over to a cupboard and opens it. It is full of files, which he contemplates with awe. He selects one.

'Judge's Decision To Terminate Inquiry Into Death At Police Headquarters . . .' (*Flicks through it.*) 'Unwarranted suspicions surrounding the fall of anarchist subversive blah from the fourth floor window. . .'

The telephone rings. The **Maniac** *casually answers it.*

Maniac   Hello, Inspector Bertozzo's office. Who are you? No, sorry, I can't put him on unless you tell me your name. You are . . . Inspector . . . No! Not really, not in person? What a total delight. Inspector Throws-Anarchists-Out-The-Window – Nothing, nothing . . . Where are you phoning from? Of course, silly me, the fourth floor – where

else? What do you mean, who am I? Guess. Oh go on, you
should always make time for fun. Come on, guess or I won't
let you speak to Bertozzo. 'Andrews?' (*To himself.*) Do I feel
like an Andrews? (*Into the phone.*) Yup, that's me all over –
Peter Andrews, good guess. 'What am I doing here at
HQ . . . ?' Rather than me tell you that, why don't you tell
me what you want Bertozzo for? No, he can't come to the
phone – tell me. 'High Court judge being sent to reopen the
inquiry', uh huh. Right, because . . . ? 'The government
obviously think the judge screwed up when he halted the
investigation into the death of the anarchist.' Well they've
changed their tune. 'Do I think they realise they made an
honest mistake?' Oh, don't make me laugh. There you go,
you've set Bertozzo off. (*He holds the receiver away and laughs.*)
Ha – now he's making obscene gestures at you. Ha ha.
(*Pretending to call over.*) Bertozzo, our friend on the fourth floor
says it's easy for you to laugh because you're not up there –
he and the superintendent are in deep shit. Ha ha. (*Into
phone.*) He says, well, keep your chin up then. Ha ha. No,
that's me laughing this time. No, because I'd genuinely love
the chief inspector to be deep in shit. Yes, you can tell him.
'Peter Andrews would genuinely love . . .' Bertozzo agrees
with me, this is him laughing. (*Holds the receiver away.*) Ha ha.
Did you hear? And nobody really cares if you get dipped in
shit and fried either. Yes, tell him this: Andrews and
Bertozzo don't give a monkey's. (*He does a huge raspberry.*)
Prrrrr. Yes, he did a raspberry. Now, come on, there's no
need *ever* to scream. Great! We'll talk about it when we next
meet. All right, what do you need from Bertozzo? Okay, I'm
writing it down: 'copy of the Judge's Report, and witness
statements'. Fine, it's all here, I'll let you have that.

So, you and your boss are doing a bit of homework before
your grilling. By the way, is it true your boss used to run a
mercenary outfit in Bosnia in the 1990s? What a sweetie!
They say this judge who's coming is as much of a bastard as
he is . . . Who says? Everyone says. Justice Malcolm. You
don't know him? You will. Funnily enough he's a liberal
colonial type and he's got a bee in his bonnet about that

whole soldiers-of-fortune-people-killing-other-people-for-money thing. So do mention that to your boss. No, maybe you'd better not – he might have you shot. Ha ha . . . Ooh, my God, you are *so* touchy up there on the controversial fourth floor.

All right, I'll bring the files up. See you – no, wait, wait. Ha ha. The Inspector's just said a very funny thing. Promise you won't get cross. Okay, I'll tell you. He said – I love his playfulness – that by the time this new judge has put you through it, you'll be kicked up north to somewhere like Huddersfield – police station all on one floor, just to be on the safe side. Inspector's office in the basement, ha ha. Do you see what I'm saying there: basement, no windows to . . . Ha ha! Did you like that one?! You didn't. Oh well, maybe it was my timing. (*Pretends to listen to voice on phone, then.*) Okay, I'll tell him: Bertozzo – the shortly-to-be-Huddersfield-based inspector on the other end of the line – says that when he sees us next he's going to punch us in the face. Message received. Roger. Prrrr! (*Raspberry.*) And goodbye.

The **Maniac** *hangs up the phone then immediately rummages through the files.*

Maniac 'To work, you old judge you – we're in a bit of a hurry.' At last, my chance to take my place among the Great and the Good. I feel rather emotional actually. This is quite a test. If I manage to convince them I'm a High Court judge . . . wow. Although if I get it wrong, I may well be in a bit of trouble . . . Let's see, first things first, let's get the walk right. (*He tries out a walk with a slight limp.*) No, that's more court usher-y. Arthritic but dignified – there we go, neck bent over, going for that 'retired circus horse' look. (*Tries another but abandons it.*) No. How about . . . more of a gliding motion with a little shake at the end? (*He tries it.*) Not bad! And the old 'knee trembler' . . . (*He tries it.*) Or stiff-legged, grasshopper-style. (*He tries it: short rapid steps rocking from heel to toe.*)

Glasses? No, no glasses. Right eye a bit sleepy . . . I'm getting there . . . Looks boss-eyed when he reads, doesn't say much . . . Slight cough – cough, cough! No, no cough. Bit of an old smoothie, nasal. Jolly in spite of an alarming twitch? No, my dear Superintendent, stop right there, you're not running Soldiers'R'Us now, if you'd just bear that in mind.

No, best go for the opposite: stand-offish, droning voice, hangdog, short-sighted, Bond-villain-style monocle.

He has been trying this out as he sorts through the files for what he wants.

Maniac   Aha!! Exactly what I'm looking for! Whoa, calm down, don't get over-excited or you'll slip out of character. (*Clipped.*) All present and correct? Let me see . . . Judge's report . . . Inquiry into suspect anarchist group led, it would seem, by a male dancer . . . Bloody marvellous!

The **Maniac** *stuffs all the documents into his bag. He takes a dark overcoat and black hat off a clothes rack and puts them on.* **Bertozzo** *enters and fails to recognise the* **Maniac**. **Bertozzo** *looks momentarily baffled.*

Bertozzo   Hello, can I help you? Are you looking for someone?

Maniac   No, Inspector, I've just come back for my papers.

Bertozzo   Get out!

Maniac   Please don't take your personal problems out on me –

Bertozzo   Out!!

He pushes the **Maniac** *to the door.*

Maniac   For God's sake! What's the matter with you all in here – is there a problem with stress? It's bad enough that madman going round looking for you to smash your face in.

Bertozzo (*stopping*)   Who's looking for me?

Maniac   Some bloke. Hasn't he punched you yet?

Bertozzo   Me? Why?

Maniac   Because you blew him a raspberry.

Bertozzo   Did I?

Maniac   Yes. Two, in fact, over the phone, and you added a nasty little laugh – ha ha. Don't you remember: ha ha. (*Mimes holding the receiver away as before.*)

Bertozzo   What are you talking about? Is this another one of your characters?

Maniac   Yes it is. I always start with the shoes. Let's just say, you'll recognise him when his fist hits your face. And I can't say I blame him.

Bertozzo   Who?

Maniac   Your neighbour up on the fourth floor. You just told him you hope he's posted to a bungalow-style police station up north alongside his boss, the ex-military personnel wholesaler and closet fascist.

Bertozzo   Who, our superintendent?

Maniac   Good, you're following. To be fair, it is complicated.

Bertozzo   Okay, zip it up, you've wasted enough of my time already. Go away and don't come back.

Maniac   Any chance of a goodbye hug? (*Seeing* **Bertozzo***'s irritation.*) Fine, I'm off. Anyway, word of advice, because I've become fond of you, if you run into an angry-looking detective from upstairs – duck.

He exits. **Bertozzo** *sighs heavily then goes over to the coat rack. It is empty. He runs after him.*

Bertozzo   Son of a bitch! Oi, you. (*He stops the* **Constable** *who is coming in.*) Run after that madman who was just in here. He's run off with my coat and hat. Quick!

Constable   Right away, Inspector.

He stops at the door. There is someone just outside the door, whom he talks to.

Constable   Yes, sir, the inspector's here.

He turns back to **Bertozzo***, who is rummaging in search of the papers torn up by the* **Maniac***.*

Bertozzo   Where have the bloody charge sheets gone?

Constable   Excuse guv, the inspector from the fourth floor is here to see you.

Bertozzo *gets up from his desk and heads for the door on the right.*

Bertozzo   Hi, I was just talking about you with some lunatic who told me (*He chuckles.*) – is this mad or what? – that when you see me you're going to give me a –

An arm shoots out from the doorway, hitting **Bertozzo** *in the face.* **Bertozzo** *is knocked to the ground, flattened. He manages to gasp:*

. . . punch in the face.

He collapses. The **Maniac** *appears at the other door and shouts:*

Maniac   I told you to duck!

Scene Two

Blackout.

The lights go up on an office very much like the last one. Furniture is more or less the same, though arranged differently. The back wall is dominated by a large portrait of the Queen. The eye is drawn to a large, wide-open window. The **Maniac** *is standing there, stock still, facing the window, but inside this time. His back is to the door through which another* **Inspector** *now enters. He is massaging his right hand. He addresses a* **Constable** *who is standing motionless at the door.*

Inspector   Who's he? What does he want?

Constable 2   I don't know, sir. He strutted in with all the confidence of . . . God. He says he wants to speak to you and the superintendent.

Inspector (*still massaging his hand, he smarms up to the* **Maniac**)   Good morning, how can I help you? I gather you're looking for me.

Maniac (*barely reacting, lifts his hat half an inch by way of greeting*) Good morning. (*He stares at the hand which the* **Inspector** *is still rubbing.*) What's wrong with your hand?

Inspector   Um. Nothing. Who are you?

Maniac   If it's nothing, why are you rubbing it? What is it, an affectation? Some kind of nervous tic?

The **Inspector** *starts to lose his cool.*

Inspector   Possibly. I asked you who I have the pleasure of –

Maniac   I used to know a bishop who rubbed himself like that. A Jesuit.

Inspector   Correct me if I'm wrong, but if you're suggesting – ?

Maniac   Of course you're wrong if you're trying to insinuate that I was alluding to the proverbial hypocrisy of the Jesuits! I was taught by Jesuits. Do you have any objections?

Inspector (*flustered*)   No . . . for heaven's sake, come on –

Maniac   Although that bishop *was* a hypocrite. Complete bloody liar, in fact. And sure enough, he was always rubbing his hand –

Inspector   Look, you –

Maniac   You should see a psychoanalyst. Compulsive rubbing of your own body is a classic sign of insecurity . . . guilt, obviously . . . and sexual inadequacy. Do you have problems with women?

Inspector (*snapping*)   That will do!

He bangs his fist on the table.

Maniac   Ah, a hot-head. So the hand-rubbing's not so much a tic as pain-relief from recently punching someone. Confess!

Inspector   What? Would you mind telling me who – And start by taking off your hat!

Maniac   You're right. (*He removes his hat with studied slowness.*) I wasn't being rude. It's that open window. I hate draughts, especially round my head. Don't you? Ghastly. Can we close it?

Inspector (*drily*)   No, we can't.

Maniac   Ooh, excuse me. I am Lord Justice Malcolm, first counsel to the High Court.

Inspector   You're a judge? (*Caught in headlamps.*) I see.

Maniac (*ironic, aggressive*)   What do you see?

Inspector   Nothing.

Maniac   How true. You see nothing! Who tipped you off that I was coming to re-examine the facts surrounding the death of the anarchist?

Inspector (*back against the wall*)   Ah, well, you see, I . . .

Maniac   Resist the temptation to lie. I find liars terribly annoying. I have a nervous tic, too. It gets me right here, at the neck. If someone lies to me, it – did you see that?! A twitch! So . . . did you know I was coming or not?

Inspector (*swallowing nervously*)   Yes, I knew. But I didn't expect you quite so soon.

Maniac   That is precisely why the High Court decided I should come early. We have informants as well, you know. So we find you unprepared, do we? Does that bother you at all?

Inspector (*now totally bamboozled*)   Not in the slightest. (*The* **Maniac** *points to his neck, which is twitching.*) Or rather . . . yes it does. A lot. (*Offers him a chair.*) Do sit down. Shall I take your hat . . . ?

Maniac   Yes, please do, it's not mine anyway.

Inspector   What? (*He goes over to the window.*) Do you want me to shut the window?

Maniac   No no, don't go to any trouble. In fact would you call the superintendent. I want to get on right away.

Inspector   Of course. Shall we go to his office? It's more comfortable.

Maniac   No doubt, but the sickening incident involving the anarchist took place in this room, didn't it.

Inspector   Yes it did.

Maniac (*spreads his arms*)   Well then!

He sits down and takes out some documents. We now have a good look at his bag, a huge one, from which he removes various odds and ends: a magnifying glass, pliers, a stapler, a judge's gavel and a copy of the Penal Code. Over by the door, the **Inspector** *mutters something to the* **Constable**.

Maniac (*continuing to sort out his files*)   Whenever I'm in the room, Inspector, I would prefer it if you spoke up.

Inspector   Of course, sorry. (*Turning to the* **Constable**.) Please ask the superintendent to come here right away, if he can.

Maniac   And even if he can't.

The **Inspector** *hesitates, looking browbeaten.*

Inspector   Yes, even if he can't.

Constable 2 (*leaving*)   Yessir.

The **Inspector** *watches the 'Judge' as he sorts out his files. He has pinned a few sheets up on the side wall, the window frame and the wardrobe. The* **Inspector** *suddenly remembers something.*

Inspector   Oh God – the statements. (*He picks up the telephone and dials a number.*) Hello, Inspector Bertozzo please . . . Where's he gone? To see the superintendent?

He hangs up and is about to dial another number. The **Maniac** *interrupts him.*

Maniac   If I might just interrupt, Inspector –

Inspector   Yes, Your Honour –

Maniac   The Inspector Bertozzo you just mentioned, is he anything to do with the reopening of the inquiry?

Inspector   Yes, well, he has the archive containing all the paperwork.

Maniac   That's not necessary. I have everything here. We don't need copies, do we?

Inspector   You're right, no, we don't.

An angry-sounding **Superintendent** *is heard outside, approaching. He bursts in, followed by an awkward-looking* **Constable**.

Superintendent   Inspector, what's all this nonsense about me having to come to see you, even if I can't?

Inspector   No, you're right, Super. The thing is though –

Superintendent   'The thing is though' fanny! Are you giving me orders now, is that it? I tell you right now that I won't put up with disrespect of this sort, especially to your colleagues. Punching people in the face, for example.

Inspector   Ah, be fair, Super. I bet Bertozzo didn't mention his joke about low-rise police stations in Huddersfield and the raspberries . . .

The **Maniac**, *pretending to gather up his paperwork, is hidden from view behind the desk.*

Superintendent   Raspberries in Huddersfield – what are you wittering on about? Come on, can we stop behaving like children. Everyone's watching what we do. Arsehole journalists making insinuations, spreading dirty little stories. (*The* **Inspector** *tries to draw his attention to the* **Maniac**, *who pretends not to be listening.*) Don't try to shut me up, I speak as I – Ah, him. God, yes. Who is he? Not a journalist . . . Why didn't you – ?!

Maniac (*without looking up*)   Don't be alarmed, Superintendent, I'm not a journalist. You won't find me spreading any gossip, I can assure you.

Superintendent   Thank you.

Maniac   I understand and share your concern. In fact I had already sought to reprimand your young colleague here.

Superintendent (*turning to the* **Inspector**)   Really?

Maniac   Yes, I'd already marked him out as somewhat tetchy, and I now discover from what you were saying that he's allergic to raspberries from the north of England – which, between you and me, are really rather bland, especially compared to free-range raspberries from say, Scotland or Jersey. Did you know that?

He takes the rather bewildered **Superintendent** *aside.*

Superintendent   No, I honestly didn't.

Maniac (*into his ear*)   A word in your ear, Super. Speaking as a father, this lad needs to see a good psychiatrist. I do in fact know one who is a bit of a genius. (*Slipping him a business card.*) Professor Anthony Rabbi, ex-lecturer, watch the comma.

Superintendent (*trying to get away*)   Thank you.

Maniac   Let's start. By the way, have you informed your colleague who I . . .

Inspector   No, sorry, I haven't had time. (*To the* **Superintendent**.) Lord Justice Malcolm, first counsel to the High Court.

Maniac   Oh, please, let's drop all this 'first counsel' nonsense. Let's just say 'one of the first'.

Inspector   As you prefer.

Superintendent (*reeling from the shock*)   Your Honour . . . I had no idea . . .

Inspector (*helping him out*)   His Honour is here to review the inquiry into –

Superintendent   Ah yes, of course, we were expecting you!

Maniac   You see! You see how straightforward your boss is!? No sleight of hand. Look and learn. Another generation, you see, old school.

Superintendent   Yes, old school.

Maniac   Look – do you mind if I say this? – I feel I sort of know you from somewhere. You weren't connected with the supply of freelance troops to the Balkans from June 1991 to the early snows of 1992 were you by any chance . . . ?

Superintendent (*spluttering*)   Supply of troops?

Maniac   No – what am I saying?! A senior policeman with a secret. Hardly. Right – back to business.

Superintendent   Yes.

Maniac (*shooting him dark looks*)   Mmm. (*Pointing a finger at him.*) No, no, impossible. You're hallucinating – stop it.

He rubs his eyes while the **Inspector** *quickly says something into the ear of the* **Superintendent**, *who looks even more anxious and lights a cigarette.*

Maniac   So, to the facts. According to these statements, on the evening of . . . nobody cares . . . an anarchist, a railway shunter, was in this room to be questioned about his possible involvement in the blowing up of the Bank of Agriculture, causing the death of some sixteen innocent civilians. Superintendent, you are quoted here as saying: 'The evidence points strongly in his direction.' Did you say that?

Superintendent   Yes, but that was in the early stages, Your Honour. Later –

Maniac   We are dealing with the early stages. Let's do this in the right order. 'Towards midnight the anarchist, seized by a "raptus" ' – this is still you speaking, Inspector – 'seized by a raptus, threw himself out of the window and fell to his death.' Now, what is a raptus? Bandieu describes it as an acute form of suicidal anguish which can strike even perfectly sane individuals if they are provoked to extremes of violent anxiety or desperation. Is that true?

Superintendent/Inspector   True./Absolutely.

Maniac   Right, let's see who or what caused this anxiety, this desperation. Let's re-construct what happened. Take it away, Superintendent.

Superintendent   Me?

Maniac   Yes, step right up. Would you mind describing your famous entrance?

Superintendent   I'm sorry, famous . . . ?

Maniac   The entrance that caused the raptus.

Superintendent   Your Honour, I think there's been a misunderstanding – I didn't make an entrance, it was my deputy –

Maniac   Ooh, ooh, I do hate to see people blaming their subordinates. So unattractive. Never mind, put that faux pas behind you and carry on.

Inspector   Your Honour, all we did was use a perfectly standard procedure, as practised in every police force, to draw a confession out of the suspect.

Maniac   Who asked you? Please let your superior do the talking. That is *incredibly* rude. Only speak when you're asked a question, is that clear? Superintendent, please recreate your entrance as it happened.

Superintendent   All right. It went something like this: the suspect, the anarchist, was over there where you're sitting. My deputy – I mean I, I came in, rather impetuously, I suppose.

Maniac   Excellent.

Superintendent   And I laid into him.

Maniac   I like what you're saying.

Superintendent   'My dear railway shunter stroke subversive, you'd better stop having a laugh at my expense' –

Maniac   No, no, stick to the script. (*Shows him the statements.*) There's no censorship here. You didn't say that.

Superintendent   All right, I said: 'Have you finished mucking me about?'

Maniac   Are you sure it was 'mucking'?

Superintendent   Yes, I promise.

Maniac   All right, go on.

Superintendent   'We have proof it was you who planted the bombs at the station.'

Maniac   What bombs?

Superintendent (*lowering his voice, chatty*)   I'm talking about the attack on the twenty-fifth.

Maniac   No, in the words you used that day. Imagine I am the anarchist railwayman. Go on, keep going, what bombs?

Superintendent   'Don't play silly buggers with me. You know what bombs I'm talking about – the ones you planted on the train at the main station eight months ago.'

Maniac   Did you really have proof?

Superintendent   No, this is one of the ploys we use in the police, as the inspector was explaining earlier.

Maniac   Ah ah . . . such cunning.

He slaps the **Superintendent** *on the back, rather to his surprise.*

Superintendent   But we had our suspicions. He was the only anarchist railwayman in town, so the finger obviously pointed at him.

Maniac   Absolutely, it's blindingly obvious. So if the bombs must have been put on the train by a railway worker, we can deduce that the bombs that went off at the Law Courts were planted by a judge, that the Memorial to the Unknown Soldier was bombed by a soldier, and the bomb at the Bank of Agriculture was the work of either a banker or a cow. (*Turning ugly.*) Come on, gentlemen, I'm here to carry out a serious inquiry, not to play cretinous guessing games. Get on with it! It says here: (*Reading from a sheet.*) 'The anarchist did not seem to be affected by the accusation, and was smiling in disbelief.' Who made this statement?

Inspector   I did, Your Honour.

Maniac   Well done. So he smiled. But it says here: 'The suicidal crisis was undoubtedly the result in part of a fear of losing his job, of being sacked.' How have we gone, at a stroke, from a smile of disbelief to fear? Who frightened him? Who told him he was going to lose his job?

Inspector   Well, I suppose, um, I –

Maniac   Please don't be modest about your contribution. You're not working in a girls' blouse shop. You wouldn't be coppers if you didn't like to put the boot in a bit. What are you: good cop, good cop? It's your birthright as policemen to behave like that! Let's not kid ourselves.

Superintendent/Inspector   Thank you, Your Honour.

Maniac   You're welcome. So you took it upon yourself to say to the anarchist, 'It's looking bad for you, imagine what your bosses on the railway would say if somebody told them you're an anarchist. They'd sack you and kick you out on the street.' Now that would really knock the wind out of him, because, to be honest, anarchists love their jobs. Deep down they're all a bit bourgeois. They love their little comforts: money coming in regularly, Christmas bonus, sick pay, pension, a peaceful old age. Anarchists are great ones for planning for their retirement, believe me. I'm talking about your modern-day anarchist, obviously, the jet-setting, city-hopping, pill-popping pacifist. Not your old-style anarchist, hounded from country to country. But you'd know all about hounding, Superintendent – No, what am I saying, stop it. So to sum up, you lowered the anarchist's morale, he got a bit depressed and threw himself out of the –

Inspector   If I may, Your Honour, it didn't actually happen that quickly. You're forgetting my input.

Maniac   You're so right. First you went out, then you came back, paused for dramatic effect, then said – Go on, Inspector, run through your lines. Imagine I'm the anarchist.

Inspector   Right. 'I've just had a phone call. Good news for you: your friend – sorry, comrade – the dancer chap, has confessed. He's admitted planting the bomb in the bank.'

Maniac   How did the railwayman take it?

Inspector   Badly, to be honest. He went pale, asked for a cigarette, lit it . . .

Maniac   And threw himself out of the window.

Inspector   Not immediately.

Maniac   You originally said 'immediately', didn't you.

Inspector   Yes I did.

Maniac   You also told the press and the television that before his tragic final act the anarchist felt lost and 'in a tight spot'. Did you say that?

Inspector   Yes, that's exactly what I said: 'in a tight spot'.

Maniac   What else did you say?

Inspector   That his alibi, to the effect that he'd spent the afternoon of the attack playing cards in his local, had collapsed.

Maniac   In other words the anarchist was strongly suspected of bombing both the bank and the trains. And you finished by calling the anarchist's suicide 'obviously the act of a guilty man'.

Inspector   I did say that, yes.

Maniac   So you blurted out to the world that he was a criminal and a piece of scum. Yet only a few weeks later, Superintendent, you stated – here's the document – that 'naturally' – let's hear that again: 'naturally' – there was no concrete proof to implicate the railwayman. Correct? So he was completely innocent, to the extent that you, Inspector, commented that 'the anarchist was a good lad'.

Superintendent   Yes, to be fair, we made a mistake.

Maniac   Well, we all make mistakes. And you, I'm here to tell you, established a new Olympic standard in mistake-making. Well done. First you arrest a blameless civilian just for the hell of it, then you abuse your authority by holding him longer than is legally permissible, then you traumatise this poor railway shunter by telling him you can prove that he's partial to blowing up railway stations. You go on to deliberately whip him into a frenzy of anxiety about losing his job, then you tell him his alibi that he was playing cards has collapsed. Then you administer the final *coup de grâce*: his friend and comrade has confessed to the massacre of innocents in a bank. His friend is a loathsome mass-murderer! At which point he says gloomily, 'This is the end of anarchy' and throws himself out of the window!

Excuse me, but are we all mad? Why are we surprised that a man who has been so abused experiences a bit of a 'raptus'? I'm sorry, but in my opinion you are as guilty as a Happy Meal! You are totally responsible for the death of the anarchist. You should be charged here and now with inciting him to kill himself!

Superintendent   Please be realistic. Our job is to interrogate suspects, you said so yourself. And in order to make them talk, from time to time we need to use stratagems, little traps and a certain amount of psychological warfare –

Maniac   Er, no – this wasn't 'a certain amount', it was an onslaught! For a start, did you or did you not have absolute proof that this poor railway worker lied about his alibi? Answer me!

Superintendent   No, not absolute proof, but –

Maniac   I'm not interested in 'but's. Is it or is it not the case that there are two or three old-age pensioners who can confirm his alibi?

Inspector   Yes, there are.

Maniac   So you lied on television and in the papers when you said that his alibi had collapsed and the evidence was stacked up against him. Not content with using these little cheats, scams and whoppers to trip up suspects, you then use them to sabotage the good faith of a gullible and gormless public. (*Ignoring the* **Superintendent**'s *attempt to object.*) Please let me finish. Hasn't anyone ever told you that giving out false or misleading information is a serious offence?

Superintendent   In fact, my officer assured me that –

Maniac   Stop dumping on people! Answer this, Inspector – where did you get the information that the anarchist dancer had confessed? I've read all the transcripts of interviews carried out by the police and the investigating judge . . . (*He shows them to everyone present.*) And nowhere does the aforementioned anarchist admit to being involved in bombing the bank. So did you make up that confession as well? Answer!

Inspector   Yes, we made it up.

Maniac   That is . . . inspired. You two should take up creative writing. In fact, you may well get the chance in prison. Always been a marvellous place to write. Okay, you're probably feeling a little bit depressed right now. So what better time to add that there is damning proof of gross negligence on your part, that you're both dead in the water, and that in an attempt to make the rest of the police look good the Home Office are going to crucify you.

Superintendent   I don't believe it!

Inspector   How can they –

Maniac   So your careers are ruined, but that's politics for you. You police were useful at first. But the mood has changed. People are angry about the death of the flying anarchist. They want to see a couple of heads roll . . . and, hey, here are two!

Superintendent   They want our heads?

Inspector   Yes!

Maniac   There's an old saying: 'The squire sets his dogs on the peasants. The peasants complain to the king, so the squire kills the dogs and gets off the hook.'

Superintendent   You don't really think –

Maniac   Who am I if not your executioner?

Inspector   What a shit job.

Superintendent   I know who's trying to destroy us, and he is going to pay for this.

Maniac   I can't deny that there will be many, many people who'll enjoy your downfall. In fact, I predict open sniggering.

Inspector   Starting with the lads here, including that one who really pisses me off.

Superintendent   Not to mention journalists.

Inspector   We are dead. We'll be all over the papers.

Superintendent   God knows what they'll come up with, these worms. They used to lick our hands, now it'll be: 'Oi, pig, oink!'

Inspector   'He's a sadist, he's violent . . .'

Maniac   And let's not forget the degradation and the never-ending sarcasm.

Superintendent   Nobody will look us in the face. We'll be lucky to get a job as car-park attendants.

Inspector   The world is . . . a bastard.

Maniac   No, the government's the bastard.

Superintendent   So what do you think we should do? Any advice?

Maniac   Me? What can I tell you?

Inspector   Advise us.

Maniac   If I were you . . .

Superintendent   Good, yes . . .

Maniac   I'd throw myself out of the window.

Superintendent/Inspector   What?

Maniac   Well, think of the humiliation you'll save yourself. Be brave! Surrender to the 'raptus' and jump, go on.

He pushes them towards the window.

Superintendent/Inspector   No, wait!/Wait a minute!

Maniac   What do you mean 'wait'? For what? There's nothing for you here on this dump of a planet. What kind of a life is this? Bastard world, bastard government! It's all . . . bastardly. In fact let's all jump!

He drags them over forcefully.

Superintendent   No, Your Honour, think about what you're doing. I still have hope.

Maniac   No, there's no more hope. Don't you get it? Hope has left the building! Jump!

Superintendent/Inspector   Help! Don't push. Please.

Maniac   I'm not pushing you, it's the raptus. The raptus will set us free!

He grabs them by the waist and forces them up on to the window ledge.

Superintendent/Inspector   No. No! Help! Help!

The **Constable** *who was there at the beginning of the interview comes in.*

Constable 2   What's happening, sir?

Maniac (*loosening his hold*)   Ha. Nothing. Everything's fine here. Isn't that right, Inspector? Super? Reassure the constable here.

Superintendent (*getting down, quivering with fear*)   Yes. Um. Relax. It was just . . .

Maniac   A 'raptus'.

Constable 2   A raptus?

Maniac   Yes, they were trying to throw themselves out of the window.

Constable 2   What, them? Really?

Maniac   Yes, but don't tell any journalists, for God's sake.

Constable 2   No, no.

Inspector   That's not true – it was the judge who was doing it.

Constable 2   You were trying to jump out, Your Honour?

Superintendent   No, he was trying to push us out.

Maniac   Oh, *that*, yes, that's true. They were nearly desperate enough to do it. When you're desperate, it takes very little to push you over the edge.

Constable 2   Tell me about it!

Maniac   Look at them, the picture of doom and gloom. All the fun of a firing squad.

Constable 2 (*excited by having the* **Maniac***'s ear*)   Pardon my French – they look like they're waiting to be flushed away.

Superintendent   Excuse me, have you gone off your head?

Constable 2   Sorry, I just meant, you looked . . . flushed.

Maniac   Yes, pull the chain! Let's end it all! Give us a smile, officers!

Superintendent   I don't think you understand the gravity of our . . . There was a moment back then when I seriously thought of throwing myself out.

Constable 2   *Yourself*, sir? I think you mean somebody else.

Inspector   No, me too!

Maniac   You see. Now you know what they mean by raptus. And whose fault would that have been?

Superintendent   Those bastards in the government. First they ask you to help – 'Ferment a little subversion, chip in with a bit of repression, go on, spread a sense of gathering disorder . . .'

Inspector   '. . . then sit back and wait for calls for a state clampdown!' So you get stuck in, and then . . .

Maniac   No, that's rubbish, it was my fault entirely.

Superintendent   Why yours?

Maniac   Because none of it's true, I made it all up.

Superintendent   What are you saying? So the Home Office don't want to crucify us?

Maniac   The thought never entered their heads.

Inspector   And the damning proof?

Maniac   There is none.

Inspector   And the story about the Ministry wanting our bollocks in their trophy cabinet?

Maniac   A delightful fabrication. The Ministry adores you. You're the apples of their eye. They burst into tears at the sound of your name.

Superintendent   Tell me you're not joking.

Maniac   The whole government loves you. I also made up that saying about the squire who kills his dogs. No squire has ever killed a dog just to keep a peasant happy. The opposite happens, if anything: if a dog dies in a fight, the king sends a telegram of condolence to the squire. And a massive wreath.

The **Inspector** *shapes up to speak. The* **Superintendent** *is nervous and hesitant.*

Inspector   So have I got this right – ?

Superintendent   Of course you haven't. Let me do the talking.

Inspector   I'm sorry, Super, of course.

Superintendent   Your Honour, I don't understand why you made up all this baloney.

Maniac   Oh no, it's not baloney, it's just the usual traps and scams that we in the judiciary use occasionally to remind the police how barbaric and of course illegal those methods are.

Superintendent   So you still believe that the anarchist threw himself out of the window because we drove him to it?

Maniac   Well, you proved as much just now, when you panicked.

Inspector   But we weren't there when he jumped. Ask him.

Constable 2   Yes, Your Honour, they left just before he jumped.

Maniac   That's like saying that someone who plants a bomb in a bank then leaves isn't guilty because he wasn't there when it went off. That has all the logic of a bag of snakes.

Superintendent   No, this is all arse about face. The constable is referring to the first version. We're talking about the second.

Maniac   Ah yes, you sort of retracted what you'd said and had another bash.

Superintendent   Well, I wouldn't call it a retraction. It was merely a correction.

Maniac   Very good. What did you 'correct'?

The **Superintendent** *signals to the* **Inspector**.

Inspector   Well, we –

Maniac   I should warn you that I have your statements for this new version. Okay, let's hear it.

Inspector   We amended the time of the . . . what shall we call it? . . . the ploy we used.

Maniac   What do you mean?

Superintendent   We stated that our session with the anarchist started at eight o'clock in the evening –

Inspector   That would be twenty hours.

Superintendent   – rather than at midnight –

Inspector   Twenty-four hours. Or is it zero zero hours.

Maniac   Right, so you brought everything forward by four hours, including the departure time from the window. A kind of Daylight Saving Gone Mad.

Inspector   No, the jump was still at midnight. There were witnesses.

Superintendent   Including the journalist who was standing in the courtyard, you remember?

Maniac *shakes his head.*

Superintendent   The one who heard the thud as the body hit the ledge then the ground, and ran over. He made a note of the time.

Maniac   Right, so your massive lying binge was at eight o'clock and the suicide happened at midnight. So where does that leave us with the raptus? Your whole account of the suicide, until proven otherwise, is based on the raptus. Everyone, from the investigating judge to the public prosecutor, had insisted from the start that the poor man jumped because of a '*sudden* raptus' and now – da-dah! – you're saying there was no raptus.

Superintendent   No, we're not, oh no.

Maniac Yes, you are! There's now a gap of four cocking hours between the moment you or some colleague came in and played your hilarious 'we have proof' joke and the suicide. And a *sudden* raptus. Four hours later? In your piggy dreams! The anarchist had had long enough to recover from that drivel by then. You could have told him that Mikhail Bakunin, founding father of revolutionary anarchism, was a pimp and ran errands for the police, and he would have had time to cheer up.

Superintendent That was exactly our intention, Your Honour. To show that the raptus couldn't have been caused by our little campaign of misinformation *precisely* because four hours went by until the suicide.

Maniac You are so right! That is beautiful thinking. Well done.

Superintendent Thank you.

Maniac So nobody can implicate you. You told a pack of evil lies but they are no longer relevant to the inquiry.

Inspector That is correct. So we are innocent.

Maniac You are tremendous. It's still not clear why the wretched man threw himself out of the window but that isn't important. What matters right now is that you are innocent.

Superintendent Many thanks again. To be honest I was afraid you'd be a bit anti us.

Maniac Anti?

Inspector Yes, that you'd be desperate to find us guilty.

Maniac Oh, please. The opposite is true. If I've come across as at all confrontational that was only to provoke you into providing me with arguments and evidence that will allow you to emerge victorious.

Superintendent I'm actually quite moved. It's nice to know that the judiciary is still the policeman's best friend.

Maniac   Or 'collaborator' . . .

Superintendent/Inspector   Yes./Indeed.

Maniac   But you have to collaborate with me because I can put you in an unassailable position.

Superintendent   Absolutely.

Inspector   I'd like that.

Maniac   The first thing we must prove beyond any doubt is that by the end of those four hours the anarchist had completely perked up following the infamous 'psychological collapse' referred to by the inquest judge.

Inspector   Well, there's this constable's testimony, and mine, that after being a bit down, the anarchist was feeling himself again.

Maniac   Is it in a statement?

Inspector   I think so . . .

Maniac   Yes, there it is, in the second version: The Facts, The Remake. (*Reads.*) 'The railwayman calmed down and said that in fact he no longer got on well with the former dancer.' Excellent!

Superintendent   In other words he wasn't going to lose any sleep over the news that the dancing anarchist had blown up the bank.

Maniac   So he didn't rate him, either as an anarchist or a dancer . . .

Inspector   Maybe he didn't find him sufficiently anarchic.

Maniac   I think he despised him.

Inspector   They probably had a quarrel and knocked each other about a bit.

Maniac   And let's not forget that our railwayman knew that the anarchist group was swarming with spies and police informants. He'd said to the ex-dancer: 'The police and the fascists are using you to create a sense of unrest. Your group's full of paid *agents provocateurs* who can manipulate you as they like. And it's the left who'll end up with egg on its face . . .'

Inspector   Maybe that's why they fell out.

Maniac   Yup, and the dancer had started to ignore him, which may have made our railwayman suspect him of being a *provocateur*.

Superintendent   Ah, that's possible.

Maniac   So our anarchist no longer gave a toss about him, which is why he would have felt relaxed!

Inspector   In fact, he was smiling, remember – I said that in the first version.

Maniac   We rest our case. Although there is the little problem that in the first version you said the anarchist was so depressed he 'lit a cigarette, wretched to his fingertips, a broken man, and declared (*Melodramatically.*) "This is the end of anarchy"'. This is all a bit Joan Crawford, isn't it? What got into you?!

Superintendent   It was his idea. (*Indicating the* **Constable**.) I told him – leave the Hollywood scripts to movie types, we're police officers.

Maniac   You know what I think? The only way to make your story sound coherent is to chuck it all away and start again.

Inspector   What, do a third version?

Maniac   God, no, let's just try and make the two we have sound vaguely plausible.

Superintendent   Good idea.

Maniac   So, rule number one: what is said is said, there's no going back. The facts are therefore that you, Inspector, and you-or-whoever-you're-dropping-in-it, Superintendent, had pulled your dirty little stunt, the anarchist had smoked his last cigarette and said his melodramatic final words. Now here comes the new bit: he didn't jump out of the window because it wasn't midnight, it was still eight o'clock.

Superintendent   As in the second version.

Maniac   And it's a well-known fact that railwaymen take timekeeping seriously, weather permitting.

Superintendent   So we've got plenty of time to change his mood and reschedule his suicidal feelings.

Inspector   This is so perfect.

Maniac   But what brought about the change? Time heals but there are limits. Someone must have helped him. Sometimes a small gesture . . .

Constable 2   I gave him a stick of chewing gum.

Maniac   Good work. You?

Superintendent   I wasn't there.

Maniac   No, you have to be there, this is a crucial moment.

Superintendent   Okay, I was there.

Maniac   Could we say, to kick off, that you were both moved by the anarchist's anguish?

Inspector   Yes, I have to say I was moved.

Maniac   And might we add that it saddened you to see him so aggrieved, Superintendent? You're a sensitive sort.

Superintendent   Yes indeed, I was saddened, deep down.

Maniac   Perfect. And I bet you couldn't resist putting a friendly hand on his shoulder.

Superintendent   I don't believe I did, no.

Maniac   Come on, a fatherly gesture . . .

Superintendent   Well, it's possible, I don't remember –

Maniac   You must have. Oh, go on, tell me you did.

Constable 2   He did, he did – I saw him!

Superintendent   Okay, if he saw me . . .

Maniac (*turning to the* **Inspector**)   And you gave him a little pat on the cheek. Like this. (*He gives him a pat on the cheek.*)

Inspector   I'm sorry to disappoint you but no patting took place.

Maniac   I *am* disappointed, and do you know why? Because this man wasn't just an anarchist, he was a railwayman, remember? Do you understand the significance of the word 'railwayman'? It's something that links us all to our childhood. It means . . . clockwork locomotives, electric train sets . . . Didn't you play with trains as a child?

Inspector   Yes, I had a real steam train, with real steam. A high-security armour-plated train, goes without saying . . .

Maniac   Did it go toot-toot?

Inspector   Yes, toot-toot.

Maniac   That's lovely – as you said toot-toot, your eyes lit up . . . Of course you were sorry for that man, Inspector, because in your subconscious you connected him with your train. If the suspect had been a banker, say, you wouldn't have looked at him twice, but he was a railwayman . . . Are you sure you didn't give him a pat on the cheek?

Constable 2   He did, I saw him. He did it. Two pats.

Maniac   You see. I have witnesses. And what did you say to him while you were patting him?

Inspector   Can't remember.

Maniac   I'll tell you what you said. You said: 'Come on, come on, don't lose heart – you wait, anarchy will never die!'

Inspector   I don't actually think –

Maniac   No, no, for God's sake, you said it, or I'll get cross. Look at the nerve on my neck. Did you say it – yes or no?

Inspector   Oh, all right, if it makes you happy.

Maniac   Well, say it then, I've got to have a record of it.

He starts to write.

Inspector   Um, I said . . . 'Come on, come on . . . don't let it get you down . . . you wait, anarchy will never die.'

Maniac   Great. And then you sang a song.

Superintendent   We sang a song?

Maniac   Well, obviously, by that stage you'd created such a friendly atmosphere, it was all a bit comradely, so you couldn't say no to the chance of a sing-song! Let me think, what would you have sung?

Superintendent   No, I'm sorry, Your Honour, but we really can't join in with an anarchist sing-song.

Maniac   You don't want to join in? Well, that's it, you're on your own then. Sort your own mess out. I'll record the facts just as you've described them. Do you know how that's going to look? Like a big bloody train crash. Oh yes. You say one thing, then you change your mind. You give one story, then half an hour later you come up with a completely new one. You can't even agree among yourselves. There's a police sergeant saying that the anarchist had already tried to throw himself out the window that afternoon, with you in the room, which you omitted to even mention.

Do you have any idea what people out there think of you? That you are liars and scum. Who do you think is ever going to believe you again? Apart from the judge who called off the inquiry, of course. And do you know basically why people don't believe you? Because your version of the facts is, well, it's complete cack for one thing, and it lacks any human understanding or warmth. Inspector, nobody's going to forget your crass reply to the anarchist's poor widow when she asked you why nobody had told her of her husband's death – 'Sorry, it won't happen again.' You don't feel anything. You never just let yourself go. Or laugh. Or cry. Or sing! People would forgive you all your balls-ups if they sensed there was a human heart beating somewhere . . . Two policemen letting their emotions grab them by the throat, joining an anarchist in his favourite song, just to make him happy! The public would weep with joy and shout your names from the rooftops at hearing such a story! So please, do yourself a favour . . . Sing!

Superintendent   All right, what shall we sing?

Maniac   Which are your favourite anarchist protest songs?

Superintendent   Ahh, there are so many. . .

Inspector   'Where Have All The Flowers Gone?'

They look at him.

Superintendent   What's that one protesters sing when they're being dragged off American military sites in Berkshire?

Inspector   Was it 'Riverdance'?

Maniac   Okay, this is what we're singing.

He brings out a lyric sheet for everyone to read then raps the words to 'Don't Believe the Hype' by Public Enemy, alone at first, then persuading the reluctant policemen to join in.

They start to sing more confidently, getting into it.

Lights slowly dim as the singing continues.

Act Two

The four men are still singing, as at the end of Act One, but have moved on to a melow protest song, e.g. 'Blowing in the Wind', accompanied by a soulful mouth organ. The lights fade up slowly.

The **Maniac** *hugs and shakes hands with the others.*

Maniac Sensational! You were tremendous! Well, I think we've proved that by now the anarchist must have been feeling pretty relaxed.

Inspector I go as far as 'happy'.

Maniac Of course, because he felt at home here! It was as though he was back in one of those anarchist groups where there are always more undercover policemen than bona fide anarchists.

Superintendent 'Our campaign of misinformation had only a minimal effect on the suspect's psyche.'

Maniac Right, so hold the raptus. That came later. (*Turning to the* **Inspector**.) When?

Inspector Around midnight.

Maniac Caused by . . . ?

Superintendent Well, I think it was –

Maniac No, no, for God's sake. You don't think anything. You know absolutely nothing, Superintendent.

Superintendent Ah, but I do.

Maniac *Jesus wept*, we are bending over backwards to get you out of this mess and show that you had nothing to do with the railwayman's death *because you weren't there.*

Superintendent You're right. Sorry! My mind was wandering.

Maniac   Well, make it sit down and shut up. So: superintendent absent. Inspector, however, present . . .

Inspector   Yes, I was, although I did pop out after a bit.

Maniac   Ah, the sound of another buck being passed. Now, be a nice man and tell me what happened around midnight.

Inspector   There were six of us in this room. Four constables, me and a sergeant.

Maniac   Since promoted.

Inspector   He's done some good work.

Maniac   And what were you doing?

Inspector   Questioning the anarchist.

Maniac   Still? 'What were you doing?! Spill it, sunbeam! Don't play games with me . . .' After so many hours you must have been shattered, beside yourselves with frustration.

Inspector   Not at all, sir, we were very calm.

Maniac   Sure you hadn't roughed him up a bit? Given his head a bit of a work-out?

Inspector   No.

Maniac (*mimes slapping his head*)   And slap! And pummel! And –

Inspector   No.

Maniac   Hai!

Inspector   Hai?!

Maniac   Karate. I know how excited you all are by precision violence.

Inspector   No, Your Honour. We were questioning him in a jokey manner.

Maniac   'Jokey'. Really.

Inspector   Honestly. Ask the constable.

He pushes the **Constable** *towards the* **Maniac**.

Maniac   Yeah, like anyone's going to believe him. Fortunately, that doesn't matter (*produces a file*), because it's in the written statements. So, what do you mean by 'jokey'?

Inspector   You know, joking around. We were questioning him and trying to have a laugh at the same time.

Maniac   I'm not with you – were you playing, what, party games? Twister? Was any dressing up involved?

Inspector   No, we didn't go that far, but we mucked around, did impersonations of the suspect, shared a gag or two . . .

Constable 2   We had such a laugh. The inspector here is a bit of a comedian – no, it's not immediately obvious. But when he's on form his interrogations are a total scream.

Maniac   Now I can see why they've decided to change your motto.

Superintendent   The police motto?

Maniac   Yup, the Home Office is changing it.

Superintendent   They're changing it?

Maniac   Well, they're adding to it. How does it go at the moment?

Inspector   'The Police – at the service of the citizen.'

Maniac   Right, from now on it's going to be: 'The Police – at the service of the citizen if they need a bloody good laugh.'

Superintendent   You see, now you've edged into mickey-taking.

Maniac   No, I have no trouble believing that you're jokey with your suspects. It reminds me of when I was in that little village when they were interrogating the so-called Monday Gang. Do you remember? There was a doctor, a pharmacist, even a priest involved – almost an entire village was put on trial, and acquitted. I was staying in a little hotel right next to the police station where they were doing the interrogating and almost every night I was woken up by the sound of shouting and screaming. At first I thought people were being roughed up or beaten, but after a while I realised that they were laughing. Laughing in a somewhat raucous manner: 'Ha ha, get out of here! Help, chuckle chuckle. Stop, Inspector, you're killing me!'

Superintendent   I'll ignore your sarcasm and just point out that every police officer involved in that case from the chief inspector to the newest constable were tried and found guilty.

Maniac   Absolutely, I believe the charge was grievous bodily hilarity. (*He notices that the police officers have reached the limit of their tolerance.*) I'm not joking. You have no idea how many innocent people make up stories just to get into police stations. You think they're anarchists, communists, agitators, trade unionists. In fact, they're just poor manic depressives, hypochondriacs and generally cheesed-off people pretending to be revolutionaries in order to be questioned by you. They want a few belly laughs! They're looking for a bit of joy in their lives, for God's sake!

Superintendent   I think you've just crossed the fine line from mickey-taking to ripping the piss.

Maniac   You still don't know me do you . . .

Inspector   Anyway, I swear we joked around with the anarchist that night.

Constable 2   Yes, we did – I swear too.

Maniac   Shut it, only senior officers can swear. All right, so what were all the jokes about?

Superintendent   Mainly about the anarchist who's a dancer.

Maniac   Why, because he has a limp? The limping anarchist dancer. Ha ha.

Inspector   Yes. And about . . .

Maniac   . . . the fact that apparently as a dancer one of his jobs was sewing beads on to Liberty lampshades. You're suggesting maybe he liked to take (*camp*) the odd liberty.

Constable 2   Anarchist poof!

Superintendent   Shut up!

Inspector   No, we didn't go that far.

Maniac   Oh, I think you're being modest. Anyroad, the fact is that you were being ponderously ironic at the expense of our railwayman's dancer friend, and he took offence. Is that true?

Inspector   I imagine that was true, yes.

Maniac   He jumped to his feet.

Inspector   Yes, he jumped up –

Maniac   And started to shout: 'No! I won't allow insinuations of this kind. My friend was a dancer, okay, he sewed beads, he had a limp, okay . . . But he was a man!' He then jumped up on to the windowsill, did a quick dancer's shimmy, then threw himself out.

Inspector   Yes, that must have been more or less it. Although I can't swear it. As I say, I'd just gone out.

Constable 2   I was there. I can swear it, if you like.

Maniac   No, shut up!

Superintendent   That's a bit over-sensitive, isn't it? Throwing yourself out of the window because someone's been rude about your friend.

Maniac   Ah, that's because they hit his weak spot –
anarchists are very serious about virility. Haven't you ever
read *Sex and Anarchy* by Otto Weininger? You haven't? It's a
classic.

Superintendent   But to take offence on behalf of a friend
you don't get on with any more . . .

Maniac   Yes. Thank you for reminding me. So he can't
have been miffed.

Superintendent   No!

Maniac   So he was pretending.

Inspector   Pretending?

Maniac   Well, obviously. The sly old bugger did a whole
number on being mortally offended just so he had a logical
reason for committing suicide. In fact his whole showy
kamikaze routine was designed to destroy you! He jumps. In
your innocence, you report the facts as you saw them . . . to
the press and on TV . . . and nobody believes you. Except of
course for the sweet judge who shelved the inquiry, who
writes in his report: 'The raptus was caused by "injured
pride".' Now who's going to swallow that? It's got bullshit
written all over it.

Superintendent   I agree, it looks ridiculous.

Maniac   So you're scuppered by your sheer sense of
honesty, while this spiteful little anarchist is lying in his
grave smirking!

Constable 2   Decent lad my prick!

Superintendent   Shut it.

The **Constable** *goes very quiet, like a snail retreating into his shell.*

Superintendent   I hope you won't mind me saying,
Your Honour, that I'm not *totally* convinced by your version
of the kamikaze railwayman.

Inspector   Yes, I have one or two reservations.

Maniac   Only one or two? I don't believe a single bloody word of it. It wouldn't even pass muster in a low-budget TV crime series made in a terrible hurry. I'm just trying to salvage something from your version, which manages miraculously to be even worse.

Superintendent (*rubbing himself to keep warm*)   Do you mind if I shut the window? It's got cold all of a sudden.

Maniac   Please do. It is cold, isn't it?

Inspector   Yeah, the sun's just gone down.

The **Inspector** *makes a sign to the* **Constable**, *who goes over and shuts it.*

Maniac   Of course, interestingly, on that evening the sun didn't go down.

Inspector   What?

Maniac   On the evening when the anarchist jumped out of the window, the sun never set.

The three policemen exchange blank glances.

Superintendent   I don't understand.

The **Maniac** *pretends to get annoyed.*

Maniac   It was December and the window was still wide open at midnight, so it can't have been cold. And the only way it couldn't have been cold is if the sun hadn't set. It must have set later, at one o'clock, like in Norway in July.

Superintendent   No, they'd only just opened it, to get a bit of air into the room, am I right?

Inspector   Yes, there was a lot of smoke.

Constable 2   The anarchist smoked a lot.

Maniac   So you'd opened the windows, but presumably not the shutters.

Inspector   Yes, and the shutters.

Maniac   In December? At midnight with the thermometer plummeting below zero and a thick fog descending? What – 'We need air, we need air! Come and get me, pneumonia!' – kind of thing? So you must have been wearing coats?

Inspector   No, just jackets.

Maniac   Snazzy!

Inspector   It wasn't cold, honestly.

Superintendent   No, it wasn't cold.

Maniac   No? That evening the weather forecast for the whole of the country was for temperatures low enough to freeze the bollocks off a polar bear. But you lot weren't cold. 'Springtime!' What was your secret – your own personal African monsoon kit? You've diverted the Gulf Stream through the sewers under the police station?

Inspector   I'm sorry, I don't get it – you say you're here to help us then you spend the whole time sneering at our evidence and making us look pathetic.

Maniac   Okay, maybe I do exaggerate, and I do have a slight tendency to completely rubbish everything you say . . . That's because dealing with you is like doing one of those puzzle books bought by children and retards: 'Find the thirty-seven mistakes made by Inspector Barry Stupidhead.' How am I supposed to help you?

The policemen are sitting there looking subdued and dismal.

Maniac   Oh, come on, don't look so bummed out. Life goes on. I promise I won't make fun of you any more. Maximum seriousness. Let's move swiftly on . . .

Superintendent   Yes, let's.

Maniac   . . . and come to the heart of the matter: the jump.

Inspector   Yes.

Maniac   Our anarchist is seized by this raptus – we'll come back to this later and find a less dodgy reason why – leaps to his feet, takes a run-up . . . Hang on, who gave him a leg-up?

Inspector   A leg-up?

Maniac   Yes, which of you stood at the window with your fingers interlaced, at about waist-height – like this – for him to put his foot in? Then: zoom! One heave and he's out over the railing and flying!

Inspector   Your Honour, I hope you're not suggesting that we –

Maniac   No, calm down, I was just wondering how anyone could get up so high with such a short run-up without any help . . . I'd *hate* anyone to get the wrong idea.

Inspector   There's no wrong idea to get – he did it all by himself.

Maniac   There wasn't one of those mini-trampolines lying around.

Inspector   No.

Maniac   Was the anarchist wearing bouncy rubber shoes by any chance?

Inspector   No, normal shoes.

Maniac   Okay, what have we got . . . A man of about five foot three, acting alone, without a stepladder. And half a dozen coppers, standing a few feet away, one of them right next to the window, none of whom manage to intervene in time . . .

Inspector   It all happened so quickly . . .

Constable 2   And he was a slippery bugger, like a bloody poltergeist! I only just managed to catch hold of his foot.

Maniac   Ah, you see how my system of goading you mercilessly works! So you caught him by the foot.

Constable 2   Yes, but his shoe came off in my hand and he proceeded in a downwardly direction without me.

Maniac   Not to worry. The main thing is that a shoe remained behind. That shoe is incontrovertible proof that you wanted to save him!

Inspector   Incontrovertible, there you go.

Superintendent (*to the* **Constable**)   Well done.

Constable 2   No problem, sir –

Superintendent   Shut up.

Maniac   Hang on, though . . . Something's not quite right here. (*Holding up a sheet of paper.*) Had the suicide victim been wearing three shoes?

Superintendent   Three shoes?

Maniac   Yes, one remained in the policeman's hands, as he testified later. (*Shows sheet.*) Here. Yet in this other document we learn that as he lay dying on the pavement the anarchist was wearing two shoes. That was confirmed by a number of bystanders including the reporter who arrived on the scene first and several other passing journalists.

Inspector   I don't know how that happened.

Maniac   Nor do I! Unless the policeman here had rushed down the stairs to a second-floor landing, got to a window just as the anarchist was plummeting, put his shoe back on *in flight*, then hared back upstairs, reaching the fourth floor just as the body hit the ground.

Superintendent   You see, *you see*, sarcasm again.

Maniac   I apologise, I am hopelessly susceptible to irony. So, three shoes. Can anyone remember if he was a triped?

Superintendent   What?

Maniac   The suicidal railwayman. If he had three feet that would account for the three shoes.

Superintendent (*curtly*)   No he was not a triped.

Maniac   Don't be tetchy. Anarchists are capable of anything.

Constable 2   I'd agree with that.

Superintendent   Shut up.

Inspector   We need to find an explanation or . . . we are in deep shit.

Maniac   I've got it!

Superintendent   Let's hear it.

Maniac   One of the shoes was a bit too big, and he didn't have an insole on him, so he put on another, smaller shoe *underneath*.

Inspector   Two shoes on the same foot?

Maniac   Yes. What's odd about that? Don't you remember galoshes – those rubber overshoes people used to wear?

Superintendent   Exactly – *used to*.

Maniac   Some people still wear them. So I put it to you that the constable had in his hands not a shoe, but a galosh.

Inspector   No, that's not possible – an anarchist wouldn't wear galoshes – far too olde-worldy and conservative.

Maniac   Anarchists are actually very conservative.

Superintendent   Oh yes, I suppose that's why they're always assassinating monarchs.

Maniac   It is, actually. Paradoxically, it's a way of preserving them for ever. If you wait for your king to die in old age, all wizened, as sick as a dog, then he decays and decomposes and you're too late. Whereas if you kill them while they're fresh and attractive . . .

Inspector   I'm sorry, Your Honour, certain subjects don't seem to me to be appropriate . . .

Superintendent   Nor to me.

Maniac   Right, so we're not going with my galoshes or three-shoes ideas –

The telephone rings. Everyone freezes. The **Inspector** *answers it.*

Inspector   Excuse me. Yes, what? Hang on. (*To the* **Superintendent**.) It's the front desk, Super. There's a journalist downstairs asking for you.

Superintendent   Oh yes. I agreed to see her today. Ask if her name's Felkin.

Inspector (*into the phone*)   Is her name Felkin? (*To the* **Superintendent**.) Yes, Maria Felkin.

Superintendent   She wanted an interview. Um, I'm too busy, ask her to come back another day.

Maniac   No, bad idea. I know all about her. She's got a hell of a temper. She could really stitch you up. I'd show her up, if I were you.

Superintendent   What about your inquiry?

Maniac   Oh, that can wait – we don't need people like that as enemies, believe me.

Superintendent   All right. (*To the* **Inspector**.) Let her come up.

Inspector   Show her up to my office. (*He hangs up.*)

Superintendent   So you're off?

Maniac   Ooh no, I'd never abandon my friends, especially at times of danger.

Inspector   You're staying?

Superintendent   But not as yourself . . . ? She's a vulture! What if she finds out who you are and why you're here? She'll splash it all over her paper. It'll destroy us.

Maniac   Relax, take deep breaths. She doesn't have to find out who I am.

Inspector   No?

Maniac   No, I'll change character. Trust me, I can do it in my sleep. Who d'you fancy: criminal psychiatrist? Interpol top brass? Head of Forensic? If she tries to trip you up with some sly question, just catch my eye and I'll step in. The main thing is that you don't put your foot in it.

Superintendent   You're being very thoughtful, Your Honour. (*He shakes his hand, obviously touched.*)

Maniac   Don't call me Your Honour, please. From now on I am Captain Mark Weeny from Forensic, okay?

Inspector   But there really is a Captain Mark Weeny.

Maniac   Exactly. So if this vulture writes something we don't like, we can prove she made it all up by calling in the real Captain Weeny.

Inspector   You are a genius. Are you up to playing a captain?

Maniac   Oh yes.

Superintendent   Shh, she's here.

*The **Journalist** comes in, sexually confident and powerful looking.*

Superintendent   Miss Felkin. Do come in.

Journalist   Good morning boys. Which one of you is the superintendent?

Superintendent   Me. Pleased to meet you. We've only spoken on the telephone. Which is a shame.

Journalist   Delighted. Your desk sergeant downstairs gave me a hard time.

Superintendent   I do apologise. My fault – I forgot to tell him you were coming. Let me introduce my colleagues: Constable Chester; the inspector, who runs this office –

Journalist   Pleased to meet you, darling.

Inspector   The pleasure's all mine. (*He gives her a firm, military handshake.*)

Journalist   You're hurting me!

Inspector   I'm sorry . . .

Superintendent (*introducing the* **Maniac**, *who is busy doing something, back turned*)   And Captain . . . Captain?!

Maniac   Hello.

He is now wearing a false moustache, a black patch over one eye, and one brown glove. The **Superintendent** *stops, lost for words. The* **Maniac** *decides to introduce himself.*

Captain Mark Weeny from Forensic. Please excuse my stiff hand. It's wooden, a souvenir of the Gulf War – say what you like about Johnny Iraqi, he knows how to whip off a hand. Please, have a seat.

Superintendent   Would you like something to drink?

Journalist   No thank you. If you don't mind, I'd like to start right away. Deadlines. We're going to press tonight.

Superintendent   Fine, let's get started, we're ready.

Journalist   I've got a few questions. (*She gets out a notebook, which she scans.*) The first is to you, Inspector, forgive me if it's a shade provocative . . . I'm going to tape this. Unless you've got a problem with that . . . ? (*She takes a tape recorder out of her bag.*)

Inspector   Ah. Aha. In fact, we –

Maniac   Please, go ahead. (*To the* **Inspector**.) Rule number . . . whatever we're up to: never say no.

Inspector   What if something slips out? We can't deny it. She'll be able to prove –

Journalist   Problem, guys?

Maniac   No, not at all. The inspector was singing your praises. I gather you're a very brave lady and a staunch democrat deeply committed to truth and justice at whatever cost to yourself.

Journalist   You're far too generous.

Inspector   So off you go.

Journalist   Why do they call you the Window-Straddler?

Inspector   Window-Straddler? Me?

Journalist   Yes. Or sometimes Inspector Straddler.

Inspector   Who calls me that?

Journalist   I have a photocopy of a letter sent by a young anarchist while he was in prison around the time of the death of the railwayman. It mentions you, Inspector, and this room.

Inspector   Mm hm? What does it say?

Journalist (*reading*)   'The inspector on the fourth floor forced me to sit on the windowsill with my legs dangling out. Then he began to hassle me. "Go on, jump . . ." and wind me up: "Haven't you got the guts? Let's get it over with. What are you waiting for?" I really had to grit my teeth to stop myself giving up and just jumping . . .'

Maniac   Fantastic. Just like a scene in a Hitchcock movie.

Journalist   Please, Captain, I asked the inspector, not you. What's your answer? (*She puts the microphone in his face.*)

Maniac (*into the* **Inspector**'*s ear*)   Calm, casual . . .

Inspector   I'm not going to answer that. I've got a question for you. Do you honestly believe I made the railwayman dangle his legs out of the window too?

Maniac   Shh, don't rise to her bait. (*Humming.*) Fly away, come on, little vulture, nothing to see here . . .

Journalist   Are you by any chance trying to disrupt the interview?

Maniac   No way! I was just idly commenting. You seem to be suggesting, Miss, Ms, that we run our police station like a TV ad for washing powder – 'We put a hundred anarchists through our Window Test . . .'

Journalist (*to the* **Maniac**)   So you're the clever one, are you?

Inspector (*to the* **Maniac**)   Thanks. You got me out of shit creek, there. (*He pats him on the back.*)

Maniac   Whooa, gently . . . I've got a glass eye. (*Points to his eyepatch.*)

Inspector   A glass eye?

Maniac   And go easy when you shake my hand, it's artificial.

Journalist   On the subject of the window, the abandoned inquiry failed to include the report on the trajectory taken by the body of the presumed suicide.

Superintendent   What good would that do?

Journalist   It would establish whether, when he emerged from the window, the anarchist was still alive . . . or less than alive. In other words, if he emerged with any impetus, or fell out lifelessly and slid down the wall, which seems to be what happened. It would establish if there were fractures or lesions to the arms and hands, which was *not* the case – in other words, the presumed suicide did not put his hands out to protect himself at the moment of impact, which would have been the instinctive reaction had he been alive.

Inspector   Yes, but don't forget that we're dealing with a suicide. This man jumped because he wanted to die!

Maniac   I'm afraid I have to agree with Miss Ms. And I am impartial, as you know. They've done experiments on this. They took some people who wanted to die, got them to throw themselves out of a window, and observed that all of them, at the last moment – wump – instinctively put their hands out in front of them.

Superintendent   Oh, thank you for your support. Are you mad?!

Maniac   Yes, who told you?

Journalist   Also missing from the evidence in that inquiry, and this is even more alarming, is a tape that recorded the exact time at which an ambulance was called. According to the ambulance people the telephone call came from the switchboard here at Police Headquarters at two minutes to midnight. But all the reporters who were there at the scene said the jump took place at precisely three minutes past twelve. So the ambulance was called five minutes before the anarchist took off out of the window. Can any of you explain this curious talent for anticipation?

Maniac   Well, we often call ambulances, as it were, *just in case*, because you never know. . . And sometimes, as here, we get it exactly right.

Inspector (*giving him a slap on the back*)   Bravo!

Maniac   Mind my eye, it'll pop out!

Superintendent   I don't understand what you're accusing us of. Is it a criminal offence to think ahead? Forward planning lies at the heart of good police work.

Inspector   In any case, I'm pretty sure this is a watch problem. The reporters' watches were all slow . . . or do I mean fast . . . ?

Superintendent   Or the timing device at the ambulance station which recorded our telephone call from here was fast . . . or do I mean slow?

Constable 2   Sounds good to me.

Journalist   Not a good night for timekeeping, then.

Maniac   Well, this isn't Switzerland. In this country we set our watches as and when we want. Some people prefer to be fast, others slow. This is a country of eccentrics, we love individuality, we vomit on convention!

Inspector   Fantastic, well said!

He gives the **Maniac** *a slap on the back. We hear the sound of a glass eye bouncing across the floor.*

Maniac   See! I warned you. My eye's popped out . . .

Inspector (*getting down on all fours*)   I'm sorry. I'll get it back for you.

Maniac   I'm sorry, Miss Ms, what were we saying . . . ?

Journalist   That in this country we vomit on convention. Well, judges investigating unexplained deaths certainly do. They don't bother to gather statements from witnesses, records of crucial timings, or forensic reports on the victim's body. They don't stop to wonder why an ambulance was called before it was needed . . . Oh, what silly details! And what about the bruises on the back of the dead man's neck?

Superintendent   I wouldn't shoot your mouth off like that, if I were you.

Journalist   Is that a threat, darling?

Maniac   No, no, Superintendent. I don't believe Miss Ms is shooting her mouth off. She's referring to a version of events which I've heard several times, and which originated, strangely enough, in this building.

Superintendent   What are you talking about?

Maniac   There's a rumour going round that a few minutes before midnight one of the men interrogating the anarchist lost his rag and gave him a massive whack on the neck – remain calm, Super – half paralysing him. He was wheezing away, having trouble breathing, so they called an ambulance. In the intervening minutes they supposedly flung open the window and leaned the anarchist out a little in the hope that the cold night air would revive him. So two of them are holding the anarchist and – as I'm sure happens a lot in these cases – each one thinks the other's got him – Have you got him? No I thought you did, oh would you believe it – and, whoops, down he goes . . .

The **Inspector** *bears down on the* **Maniac,** *furious, but slips on the glass eye and falls over.*

Journalist   I'll buy that.

Superintendent   Have you gone mad?

Maniac   Yes. Sixteen times.

Inspector   What the hell did I skid on?

Maniac   My glass eye. You've got it all dirty, look. Constable would you please get me a glass of water to rinse it in.

The **Constable** *exits.*

Journalist   You must admit that this version clears up a lot of mysteries: why the ambulance was called minutes early, why the body was lifeless when it fell. And why the public prosecutor used that odd phrase in his summing-up.

Maniac   Which phrase? Please spell it out, I've got a thumping headache.

Journalist   The public prosecutor stated, in writing, that the anarchist's death should be classified as an 'accidental death'. An accident, not a suicide, as you've described it. And there's quite a difference between the two.

Meanwhile the **Constable** *has returned and handed the glass to the* **Maniac** *who, absorbed in what the* **Journalist** *was saying, takes a swig of water and swallows the glass eye.*

Maniac   Oh God! My eye! I've swallowed my eye! Oh well, let's hope it gets rid of my headache.

Superintendent (*into the 'Captain's' ear*)   What are you playing at now?

Inspector (*taking over from the* **Superintendent**)   Don't you think you've given that woman enough rope to hang us with?

Maniac   Just let me handle it. (*To the* **Journalist**.) Right, I'm going to prove to you that the version of events you describe is utterly unreliable.

Journalist   Unreliable? In the same way that the judge who wound up the inquiry described evidence given by the old-age pensioners as unreliable?

Maniac   I sense you want to talk to me about unreliable pensioners.

Journalist   The anarchist claimed he'd spent the tragic afternoon of the bombing in a bar by the canal playing cards with three regulars. In his summing-up the judge dismissed the evidence of these three witnesses on the grounds that they were unreliable.

Maniac   Why were they unreliable?

Journalist   Because, according to the judge, 'these people are old, a bit shaky on their feet and basically disabled'.

Maniac   The judge wrote that in his summing-up?

Journalist   Yes.

Maniac   Well, you can't argue with that, can you. You can't expect a pensioner, probably carrying some hideous war wound or industrial disability – an ex-worker: *ex*, you see – to possess the minimum level of physical and mental health needed for the delicate task of giving evidence.

Journalist   What's wrong with an ex-worker?

Maniac   Come on, Ms, which planet are you living on? Instead of poncing around in Cannes or the Middle East or anywhere with a new branch of Harvey Nichols why not take a trip to West Bromwich or Strathclyde or Oldham? Do you have any idea what it's like to be a worker? When they finally reach retirement age – and according to the latest figures fewer do every year – they've been squeezed like lemons, they're zombies.

Journalist   I think you're going a bit over the top there.

Maniac   You think so? Well, pop into some bar where you've got your pensioners playing cards in a corner and have a listen. They're shouting away, slagging each other off for not remembering whose turn it is: 'Hey, loser, it was me, I put down the seven of spades.' 'No, that was in the last game.' 'What do you mean the last game, we've only just started playing, you cretinous has-been.' 'Don't you has-been me, you senile old fool.' 'Senile? Who do you think you're talking to?' 'I don't know. Do you?' 'Not a clue.'

Journalist (*laughs*)   I think you're exaggerating slightly to get a laugh. Maybe it's their fault if they end up in that pitiful state.

Maniac   No, it's society's fault. But we're not here to put capitalism in the dock, we're here to discuss whether evidence is reliable or not. Our priority is justice, we can't get sentimental about witnesses just because their jobs left them for dead or they mislaid a limb on an assembly line.

Superintendent   Well said, Captain.

Maniac   Can't afford vitamins, protein, organic honey or calcium phosphate to keep your memory sharp? Well, hard lines, I'm the judge and I'm turning you down, you're not up to it, you're a second-class citizen.

Journalist   Ah, you see, you see, I knew you'd reduce it all to class prejudice and privilege.

Maniac   Has anyone got any better ideas? I admit it, it's true, society is split into classes. And the same obviously goes for witnesses. You've got your first-, second-, third- and fourth-class witnesses. It's not a question of age. You can be frighteningly old and quite breathtakingly out-to-lunch, but if you turn up in court after a bit of work from a crack team of beauticians, a massage, a quick sesh under a sunlamp, in a silk shirt, little scarf, big chauffeur-driven Mercedes – well, then I can't quite see the judge dismissing you as unreliable. I personally would even throw in a bit of gratuitous bowing. 'Super-reliable', that would be my verdict.

He comes out from behind the desk for the first time. He is wearing a wooden leg, pirate-style. Everyone looks at him in amazement. The **Maniac** *is unfazed.*

Bosnia – terrible time. Had to amputate my own leg with a sharp rock. I don't want to talk about it, it's all water under the bridge.

The door opens. It is **Bertozzo**. *He has a bandage over one eye.*

Bertozzo   Sorry, am I interrupting anything?

Superintendent   Come in, come in, Inspector Bertozzo.

Bertozzo   I just need to leave this here.

He is holding a metal box.

Superintendent   What is it?

Bertozzo   A copy of the bomb which exploded in the bank.

Journalist   Oh my God.

Bertozzo   Don't be alarmed, madam, it isn't wired up.

Superintendent   Even so, easy . . . Put it down there. Come and shake hands with your colleague. You too, Inspector. Settle your differences, come on.

Bertozzo   I'd just like to know why he gave me a black eye.

Inspector   Yeah, like you don't know. What about the raspberry?

Bertozzo   What raspberry – ?

Superintendent   Okay, shut up, we've got visitors.

Maniac   Indeed.

Bertozzo   Sorry, do I . . . ? Your face is familiar.

Maniac   Could that be because . . . we've both got eye trouble?

Everyone laughs.

Bertozzo   No, seriously . . .

Maniac   I'm sorry . . . I'm Captain Mark Weeny from Forensic.

Bertozzo   You can't be. I know Captain Weeny.

Superintendent (*giving him a little kick*)   No you don't.

Bertozzo   What do you mean I don't know him?

Inspector   You don't know him. (*Also kicks him.*)

Bertozzo   Don't you start.

Superintendent   Just drop it, okay? (*Another kick.*)

Bertozzo   We trained together –

*He receives another kick, this time from the **Maniac**.*

Maniac   They told you to drop it! (*He gives him a smack on the head.*)

Bertozzo   Oi!

Maniac (*pointing to the **Inspector***)   It was him.

*The **Superintendent** brings **Bertozzo** over to the **Journalist**.*

Superintendent   Bertozzo, let me introduce Miss Felkin. (*To **Bertozzo**.*) I'll explain later. (*To them both.*) She's a journalist. (*Giving* **Bertozzo** *another dig in the ribs.*) With me now?

Bertozzo Inspector Bertozzo, pleased to meet you . . . No, I'm not with you.

The **Superintendent** *kicks him, then the* **Maniac** *kicks him, clearly enjoying himself. He gives the* **Superintendent** *a kick, just for the hell of it, then slaps* **Bertozzo** *and the other* **Inspector** *on the back of the neck.* **Bertozzo** *thinks it was the* **Inspector** *who did it.*

Bertozzo Look, Super, he's doing it again!

Finally the **Maniac** *pats the* **Journalist***'s bottom then points to the* **Superintendent**.

Journalist For crying out loud! Is that any way to behave?

Superintendent (*assuming she means the men's squabble*) You're right, it's a long story . . . Bertozzo, pack it in and listen. Miss Felkin is here for a very important interview, do you understand?

He kicks **Bertozzo** *then winks at him.*

Bertozzo I'm with you now.

Superintendent So, Miss, I don't know if you want to ask him any questions . . . ? Inspector Bertozzo is one of our top experts on ballistics and explosives, among other things.

Journalist Oh, there is something that intrigues me. You said that that box contains a copy of the bomb that went off in the bank.

Bertozzo Well, a very approximate copy. The original device blew up, so . . . you see our problem.

Journalist But another bomb was found that didn't go off.

Bertozzo Yes.

Journalist   So can you explain why, instead of disconnecting it and having Forensic test it thoroughly, standard practice, when they found it they took it straight out into the courtyard, buried it and blew it up?

Bertozzo   I'm sorry, what's your point?

Journalist   I think you know, Inspector. When you destroy a bomb you erase the bomber's signature.

Maniac   That's true. That's why people always say: I'm hopeless with names but I never forget a bomb . . .

Bertozzo (*shaking his head*)   That is *not* Weeny . . .

The **Maniac** *picks up the box containing the bomb.*

Superintendent   Of course it's not him, shut up!

Bertozzo   I knew it. So who is it?

He receives yet another kick.

Maniac   I wonder if Inspector Bertozzo would allow me in my capacity as Head of Forensic –

Bertozzo   Yeah, right . . . What are you doing? Please don't touch that box! It's dangerous.

Maniac (*giving him a quick kick*)   I know what I'm doing.

Superintendent   Actually, do you?

The **Maniac** *gives him a contemptuous look.*

Maniac   You see, Miss Ms, this type of bomb is so complicated – wow, look at all those wires – two detonators, timer, fuse, levers in all shapes and sizes . . . As I say, it's *so* complicated that it would be easy to hide inside it a second timing device with a delayed action, and the only way of finding it would be to dismantle it completely, which would take a whole day. During which time it could go off at any moment.

Superintendent (*to* **Bertozzo**)   Pretty convincing expert, don't you think?

Bertozzo (*dogged*)   Yes, but it's not Weeny.

Maniac   So that's why they preferred to sacrifice the perpetrator's signature, and detonate the bomb in a courtyard rather than risk it going off anywhere near the public and killing even more people than the first bomb. Convinced?

Journalist   All right, this time you have convinced me.

Maniac   Yes, I've even managed to convince myself.

Inspector   Me too! Good stuff. Nice angle of attack.

He shakes the **Maniac** *vigorously by the hand, which comes off in the* **Inspector**'s *hand.*

Maniac   You've pulled it off! I told you it was wooden.

Inspector   My mistake.

Maniac   There's only the leg to go now. (*He reattaches his hand.*)

Superintendent (*to* **Bertozzo**)   Say something, Bertozzo, just to show that we're up to speed too.

He gives him a little pat on the back.

Bertozzo   Certainly. The real bomb was in fact extremely complex. I saw it. Much more complex than this one. Some real old craftsmanship went into it. Professional job.

Superintendent   Steady . . .

Journalist   Professional . . . Or military?

Bertozzo   More than likely.

The three men all kick him.

Superintendent   You stupid bastard.

Bertozzo   What did I say?!

Journalist (*has all she needs*)   Fine. So even though you knew that assembling, or even handling, bombs of this type required professional – preferably military – expertise, you nonetheless went after one little ramshackle group of anarchists and let all other potential culprits – we all know who I mean – cover their tracks.

Maniac   Well you can't really rely on Bertozzo's interpretation because he's not a proper explosives expert. It's more of a hobby for him . . .

Bertozzo (*offended*)   A hobby?! What do you know about it? Who are you? (*Turning to the two policemen.*) Who is he? Is anybody going to tell me?

More kicks force him to sit down.

Superintendent   Please relax . . .

Inspector   Calm down . . .

Journalist   Take it easy, Inspector. I'm sure everything you've said is true, but the fact is that the police and the whole justice system jumped at the chance to incriminate – how shall I describe them? – a bunch of stunningly confused, madcap anarchists, headed by a retired hoofer.

Superintendent   They may have looked confused but that was a smokescreen.

Journalist   Really, and when the smoke cleared what did we find? Of the ten members of the group, at least two were working for you as informants, or rather spies and agents provocateurs. One of those was known by all and sundry, *except* the befuddled group itself, to be a local fascist. And the other was one of your own officers masquerading as an anarchist.

Maniac   Yes, and I don't know how the anarchists didn't see him coming – he can't *spell* anarchism let alone promote it as a rallying point for anyone disillusioned by orthodox political systems.

Bertozzo   You fucking know-it-all. God, who is he. . . ?

Superintendent   I can't agree with you, Captain. The policeman-cum-spy you referred to is an essential component in our utter preparedness.

Journalist   And do you have many more of these frighteningly prepared policemen-cum-spies beavering away inside other extra-parliamentary groups?

Maniac (*singing quietly*)   Fly away, little vulture, nothing to see here . . .

Superintendent   I'm delighted to reveal that we have, yes, lots of undercover agents, pretty much everywhere.

Journalist   Now I know you're bluffing, Superintendent.

Superintendent   Not at all. In tonight's audience, for example. We have a few of our people in. Do you want to see?

He claps his hands. Voices are heard from various points in the auditorium.

Voices   Superintendent!/Over here, sir!/Yessir?

*The **Maniac** laughs and turns to the audience.*

Maniac   Don't be alarmed, they're drama students. The real undercover ones are trained to sit quietly.

Superintendent   Informers and spies are our great strength.

Inspector   They provide an early-warning service and a means of control.

Maniac   They also carry out atrocities to give themselves a good excuse for a police crackdown. (*The police officers react with shock.*) I was just getting in before our sexy beast journalist here.

Journalist   Well, it's pretty bloody obvious. And given that you had every member of the little troupe under close scrutiny, how did they pull off such a complex bombing operation without you doing anything about it?

Maniac   Careful – vulture circling.

Superintendent   Our undercover agent could not in fact be with the group in the days prior to the bombing.

Maniac   It's true, he brought a note from his parents. Really, it's true . . .

Inspector   Please . . . (*Sotto.*) Your Honour –

Journalist   But what about the other informer, the fascist? He was there, wasn't he. . . ? In fact, the inquiry judge believed he was the real organising force behind the bombings. He exploited the anarchists' simple mindedness and lured them into an attack, the seriousness of which they didn't fully understand. I'm merely quoting the judge himself.

Maniac   The vulture has landed.

Superintendent   Well, for a start, the fascist you're talking about isn't our informer.

Journalist   Oh, come on, he had a parking space at Police Headquarters.

Superintendent   If you say so. I don't know anything about that.

Maniac   Well done, nice stonewalling. (*He goes to shake the* **Superintendent***'s hand.*)

Superintendent   Cheers.

He shakes the **Maniac***'s wooden hand, which comes off again.*

Sorry, your hand . . .

Maniac   Keep it, I've got a spare. (*Takes out a woman's hand.*)

Inspector   Isn't that a woman's hand?

Maniac   It's unisex.

Journalist (*taking papers out of a folder*)   You say you don't know anything . . . So you'll be unaware that of the 173 bomb attacks to date (*Reads from document.*) 102 have been proved to be the work of fascists? And fascist or parallel organisations were strongly implicated in half of the remaining seventy-one cases.

Maniac   Nice one.

Superintendent   Those figures may be correct, yes . . . Any comments, Inspector?

Inspector   I'd have to check.

Journalist   Good, and while you're at it check how many of those attacks were made to look like the work of far-left groups.

Inspector   Well, almost all of them, obviously.

Journalist   As you say, obviously. And how many times did you, the police, fall for it? And was that out of naivety or . . . ?

Maniac (*running his woman's hand over his face*)   That is so bitchy.

Bertozzo   I definitely know him. Right, that eyepatch is coming off.

Maniac (*ironically*)   But what do you expect, Miss, in the face of such blatant provocation? I suppose you'd argue that if we police, instead of faffing around after a bunch of no-hoper anarchists, had concentrated on pursuing other more worthwhile lines of inquiry such as fascist and paramilitary organisations financed by industrialists and run and backed by Western armed forces – then perhaps we would have sorted out this business long ago.

Superintendent (*to* **Bertozzo**, *who is getting heated*)   Don't worry, now he'll flip the whole argument on its head. He's got this technique – very gifted man.

Maniac   If you believe *that* then . . . you're right. What a waste of time! We could have uncovered a load of fantastic dirt!

Bertozzo   Okay, kill him.

Superintendent   He's gone mad . . .

Bertozzo (*getting it*)   Mad . . . Mad! He's that maniac.

Journalist   That's a bit rich, coming from a policeman.

Bertozzo (*pulling the **Superintendent** over to one side*) Super, I know who he is!

Superintendent   Yeah, well, keep it under your hat, don't spread it around.

*He walks away from **Bertozzo**, back to the **Maniac** and the **Journalist**. **Bertozzo** takes the **Inspector** aside.*

Bertozzo   Honestly, I know him. He's never been a copper. He's just dressed up as one!

Inspector   I know, we all know. We don't want the journalist to realise.

Bertozzo   But he's a crank.

Inspector   Shut up, I can't hear what they're saying.

We pick up the others' conversation.

Maniac   . . . you're a journalist so you are like a pig in shit over a good scandal like this. You don't really care if innocent people were massacred in a bank for the sole purpose of distracting the public from stories of industrial unrest last autumn, creating an atmosphere of insecurity and a sense of disgust at this political turmoil, leading to a clamour for a strong state.

Inspector   Didn't I read that in one of the big papers?

Bertozzo *comes up behind the **Maniac** and snatches off his eyepatch.*

Bertozzo   There! See – he's got an eye!

Superintendent   What are you on about, you moron, of course he's got one.

Bertozzo   So why was he wearing an eyepatch?

Inspector   You've got an eye under your patch, nobody goes round ripping yours off. (*He takes him aside.*) Behave. I'll explain later.

Journalist   That's so eccentric, you wear an eye-patch just for fun?

Maniac   No, just to blend in really.

He laughs, indicating **Bertozzo**'s *eyepatch. The* **Journalist** *laughs too.*

Journalist   Very good . . . Go on then, the scandal . . .

Maniac   Ah yes. So there's a massive scandal. Mass arrests of politicians. The odd trial. Lots of big cheeses sweating. Lords, members of parliament, colonels . . . Liberal Democrats rather overexcited and tearful. The *Mail on Sunday* sacks its editor. The Left tries to ban fascists. And finally the chief of police is carried shoulder-high through the streets for carrying out such a fearless operation. Shortly afterwards he's politely told to retire.

Superintendent   No, Captain. I don't like these gratuitous insinuations . . .

Journalist   This time I agree with the superintendent. A scandal like that would actually boost the standing of the police. The public would have an enhanced sense of well-being and a new respect for our justice system.

Maniac   Absolutely, so the scandal would have served its purpose. People say they want real justice . . . so we fob them off with a *slightly* less unjust system of justice. Workers howl that they're being flayed like donkeys . . . so we arrange for the flaying to be a *little* less severe and slash their howling entitlement, but the exploitation goes on. The workforce would rather not have fatal accidents in the factory . . . so we make it a teeny bit safer and increase compensation payments to widows. They'd like to see class divisions eliminated . . . so we do our best to bring the classes marginally closer or, preferably, just make it seem that way.

They want a revolution . . . and we give them reforms. We're drowning them in reforms. Or promises of reforms, because let's face it, they're not actually going to get anything.

Inspector   Are you aware that it's an offence to show contempt for the judiciary?

Superintendent   He's bonkers.

Bertozzo   I know he is, I've been trying to tell you for half an hour.

Maniac   You see, your average citizen doesn't want the dirt and the injustice to go away. He's just happy to see it exposed, let's all have a jolly scandal, and everyone gets something to talk about. That, for him, is what freedom means in the best of all possible worlds. Hallelujah!

pg 80

Bertozzo (*grabbing the* **Maniac**'s *wooden leg and shaking it*) Look, his leg isn't real!

Maniac   Yes it is. It's walnut.

Superintendent   It's all right, we know . . .

Bertozzo   It's a trick, it's strapped on at the knee. (*He starts to undo the straps.*)

Inspector   Oi, Bozo, leave him alone. What do you want to do, dismantle him completely?

Maniac   No, please, don't stop him. I'd lost the feeling in my thigh. Thank you.

Journalist   I wish you'd all stop interrupting. Just because his false leg is . . . false, it doesn't mean he isn't worth listening to.

Bertozzo   Even though he's a bullshitter, an obsessive hypocrite, he's never been injured in a war and he's not even a captain . . . ?

Journalist   So who is he?

Bertozzo   He's just a –

The **Superintendent**, **Constable** *and* **Inspector** *put their hands over* **Bertozzo***'s mouth and drag him away.*

Superintendent (*to the* **Journalist**)   Sorry about this, he's wanted on the telephone.

They put him down at the desk and wedge the receiver under his mouth.

Inspector (*into* **Bertozzo***'s ear*)   Are you trying to destroy us, you arse?

The **Journalist** *and the 'Captain' go on talking, ignoring the group of policemen.*

Superintendent   This is a secret – geddit? If she finds out that they've reopened the inquiry we are really screwed.

Bertozzo   There's a new inquiry – ? (*They shove the phone back under his mouth.*) Hello?

Inspector   What!? Why did you say you knew everything when you knew bugger all, you prattling halfwit? You're messing it up for everyone.

Bertozzo   I'm not! I just want to know –

Superintendent   Ring somebody, and shut up.

He bashes **Bertozzo** *on the knuckles with the phone, then hands it back to him.*

Bertozzo   Ow! Hello, how are you?

We return to the **Journalist***'s conversation with the 'Captain'.*

Journalist   . . . very funny. Superintendent, you can relax. The Captain – not that he is a captain – has told me everything.

Superintendent   What's he told you?

Journalist   Who he is.

Superintendent/Inspector   He told you?/What?

Maniac   Yes, the lying had to stop. Anyway, she'd worked it out for herself.

Superintendent   I hope she promised not to include it in her article.

Journalist   Of course I'll include it. Where are we . . . (*Reading from her notes.*) 'Bishop Reveals Himself At Top Cop Shop.'

Inspector/Superintendent   A bishop?

Maniac   Yes, I'm sorry I had to conceal my real identity . . .

He casually turns his collar round so it looks like a vicar's dog collar, to go with his black shirt.

Bertozzo (*exasperated*)   Now he's a bishop . . . Please tell me you're not going to believe him.

The **Inspector** *picks up a large rubber stamp and wedges it in* **Bertozzo***'s mouth.*

Inspector   You're getting very annoying . . .

The **Maniac** *has produced a red skullcap which he now puts on. Slowly and with great dignity, he undoes a jacket button to reveal a baroque gold and silver crucifix. Finally, he puts on a large ring with a huge purple stone.*

Maniac   Pleased to meet you. I am Bishop Bernard, police liaison officer and consultant.

He presents the ring to the **Constable***, who kisses it.* **Bertozzo** *comes forward, removing his dummy-like rubber stamp from his mouth.*

Bertozzo   Police liaison officer?

Maniac   Following some unpleasantness directed at some of our senior churchmen, it is our duty as plainclothes men of the cloth, as you can well understand, to alert the police and ensure that communication –

Bertozzo   No! *No!* Police bishops?! Stop it, come on!

The **Inspector** *puts the rubber stamp back in* **Bertozzo***'s mouth and pulls him to one side.*

Inspector   We know he's talking bollocks. He's doing it to try and save us, okay?

Bertozzo   He can't save your soul. He's not qualified.

Inspector   Shut your face and kiss his ring.

He pushes **Bertozzo***'s mouth towards the* **Maniac***'s ring. The* **Maniac** *has been nonchalantly offering his ring to everyone in the room, receiving obedient kisses.*

Bertozzo   No, for God's sake. Not the ring! I refuse. You're all out of your heads – he's spreading his sickness.

The **Inspector** *and the* **Constable** *rush over with quantities of sticking plaster which they stick roughly over* **Bertozzo***'s mouth until half of his face is covered, from the nose downwards.*

Journalist   What's the matter with him, poor man?

Maniac   Crisis of faith.

He produces a prayer book, opening it to reveal a hidden syringe, which he prepares to use on **Bertozzo**.

Maniac   Hold him down. This will do him a power of good. It's a tranquilliser made by Trappist monks.

Superintendent   What does it do?

Maniac   I'm not allowed to talk about it.

He injects **Bertozzo** *with impressive swiftness, then examines the syringe.*

There's a bit left . . . Would you like it?

Without waiting for an answer, the **Maniac** *pounces and injects the* **Superintendent***, who does a muffled groan.*

Journalist   You won't believe this – Your . . . Grace? – but just now when you were talking about the scandals and you said: '. . . in the best of all possible worlds . . . hallelujah!', I immediately thought – I don't mean to be irreverent –

Maniac   Please, please . . .

Journalist   I thought: 'Why's he talking like a bloody priest?!' I hope you're not offended . . .

Maniac   Why would I be offended? It's true, I was talking like a bloody priest, because . . . I am a bloody priest.

As the **Maniac** *speaks,* **Bertozzo** *picks up a marker pen, goes over to the portrait of the Queen hanging on the wall, turns it over and writes on the back 'He is a clinically deluded madman'. He holds the message up behind the* **Maniac***'s head for the others to see.*

Interestingly, when St Gregory the Great was elected pope he found out that they were trying by various shady means and how's-your-father to cover up some major scandals. He was furious and shouted out those famous words: '*Nolimus aut velimus, omnibus gentibus, justitiam et veritatem* . . .'

Journalist   I'm sorry, I was crap at Latin at school . . .

Maniac   Oh, fine – it basically means: 'You're going to get justice and truth, whether you like it or not. I'll do everything I can to make these scandals explode like a thousand . . . fireworks. And fear not that all this putrescence will submerge my authority. Let the scandals come, because from them will rise up a stronger, more enduring state.'

Journalist   That's amazing. Would you mind writing all that down for me?

The **Maniac** *starts to write the quote, adapted rather freely from Pope Gregory, in the* **Journalist**'s *notebook. In the meantime, the* **Inspector** *has snatched the portrait out of* **Bertozzo**'s *hands and torn it up.*

Superintendent (*laying into him*)   What are you playing at? You've destroyed the Queen's picture. That's an offence!

Inspector   He was writing on it . . . (*He points to* **Bertozzo**.)

Superintendent   I agree he was wrong to write melodramatic messages on the back of a royal portrait, but there's no excuse to do that. Shame on you!

The **Journalist** *has been standing behind the* **Maniac** *taking great interest in the words of Pope Gregory.*

Journalist   In other words, if there were no scandals they'd have to invent them.

Maniac   Exactly. Tensions massaged away through the miracle of catharsis, and you journalists are the over-indulged chief masseuses.

Journalist   Indulged? Tell that to the government – have you seen it rushing around desperately trying to suppress our stories?

Maniac   Oh, it only ever pretends to. They all get out, don't they? Cash for questions. Donations for passports. Cemeteries for a quid. Guns to Iraq. MPs caught with their adulterous cocks out while urging restraint and probity. Eighteen Jeffrey Archer scandals. Another thirty-two ending with the word 'gate'. Did the state crumble? Did the stock exchange collapse? On the contrary, they went from strength to strength. People thought: okay, something stinks here but we've brought it to the surface. We're swimming in it and even drinking some of it, but nobody's trying to pretend it doesn't exist. So that's all right then.

Superintendent   Oh, hardly, that's as good as saying that scandal is the fertiliser of social democracy.

Maniac   Brilliant! There you go: Scandal Is The Fertiliser Of Social Democracy! I'd go even further: Scandal is the best antidote to the worst poison: namely a sense of awareness. If people come to realise what's going on we are in deep trouble. Look at America, the archetypal social democracy. They never tried to cover up US atrocities in Vietnam. You're kidding: its papers were full of photographs of women with their throats cut, massacred babies, decimated villages. And do you remember the scandal of the nerve gas? This was a gas manufactured in America in large enough quantities to erase the human race three times over. Did they try to conceal this? Get out of here! You could turn on your TV and watch the cargo trains go by: 'Where are the trains going, Mummy?' 'To the sea!' 'What's in the trains?' 'Nerve gas, darling – they're burying it just a mile or two out to sea!' One little earthquake, the containers rupture, nerve gas glugs to the surface and we all die. Three times.

They've never tried to cover up these scandals. Which is great! So the public can really vent their outrage and disgust: 'What is this government thinking of!?' 'Arsehole generals!' 'Murderers!' So they get cross, then possibly even angry, but then the bubble bursts. It's like a burp. Then the meal is over.

Bertozzo   Hands up! Backs against the wall or I'll shoot!

Bertozzo *is levelling a gun at everyone in the room.*

Inspector   Bertozzo, are you crazy?

Bertozzo   Hands up, I said. You too, Superintendent. I should warn you I'm a little bit out of control.

Journalist   Oh my God.

Superintendent   Calm down, Bertozzo.

Bertozzo   No, you calm down.

He takes a pile of handcuffs out of the desk, hands them to the **Constable** *and gestures for him to handcuff all the others.*

Bertozzo   Go on, handcuff them all.

There is a high horizontal bar at the back of the stage, to which everyone in the room is handcuffed one by one, one handcuff round their wrist, the other round the bar.

And don't look at me like that. You'll understand in a minute that this is the only way I can get a proper hearing. (*To the* **Constable**, *who is hesitating.*) Yes, the lady too. And you. (*Turning to the* **Maniac**.) Whereas you, Mr Conman Wankmouth, will kindly tell the lady and gentlemen who you really are. Or, you annoying bastard, I'll shoot your face off, okay?

The policemen and **Journalist** *mutter unhappily at this display of contempt for the* **Maniac**.

Shut up.

Maniac   *Delighted* to do what you suggest but I'm a bit worried that they won't believe me.

Bertozzo   Maybe you should sing it to them then.

Maniac   No, it might be enough just to show them my file with my clinical records and all that.

Bertozzo   All right, where are they?

Maniac   In that bag.

Bertozzo   Go on, get them then. Any mucking about and you're a dead man.

The **Maniac** *takes half a dozen notebooks and files out of his bag.*

Maniac   There.

He hands them to **Bertozzo**, *who distributes them to the handcuffees to read.*

Bertozzo   There you go. Seeing is believing.

Superintendent   Noooo! An art teacher, on indefinite sick leave! Suffers from paranoid delusions . . . So he's mad.

Bertozzo (*sighs*)   Oh, didn't I mention that?

Inspector (*reading in another file*)   Has spent time in psychiatric hospitals in Broadmoor, the Maudesley, Rampton . . . Looks like he's given them all a go.

Maniac   Yep, I've done the Grand Tour for the mentally disturbed.

Journalist   Fifteen electric shock treatments . . . In solitary for twenty days . . . Three incidents of criminal damage.

Constable 2 (*reading a file*)   He's a pyromaniac! Ten arson attacks!

Journalist   Let's have a look. Burned down the library in Alexandria, Egypt. In the second century BC.

Bertozzo   Give it here. (*Reading.*) He's written that in himself, look.

Superintendent   So we can add 'forger' to hoaxer, impostor, quick-change artist . . . (*Turning on the* **Maniac**, *who is sitting with his large bag on his lap, looking innocent.*) You're going down, for . . . abusing important people!

Maniac (*shaking his head, smiling*)   Tut tut.

Bertozzo   You can't – he's a mental patient. I've been through all that with him.

Journalist   Such a shame. I was planning a fantastic article. So much for that.

Inspector   Yeah, and so much for him when I've pushed his head into his body. Bertozzo, undo these handcuffs, for God's sake.

Bertozzo   I don't think that would do you any favours . . . In India the cows are sacred, over here it's the lunatics.

Superintendent   What a skunk . . . Mental . . . Passes himself off as a judge . . . That rubbish about reopening the inquiry . . . It's all been a bit of a shock . . .

Maniac   Call *that* a shock . . . (*Calling out.*) Hello,
everybody!

From his bag he takes out the box that **Bertozzo** *had left on the table
earlier.*

Count to ten and then up we go, boom!

Bertozzo   What are you doing? Don't be a prat, now . . .

Maniac   Be careful what you say, Bertozzo, and drop
your gun. Or I'll put my finger on the detonator, here, and
off we'll all go.

Journalist   God! Please don't.

Superintendent   Don't fall for it, Bertozzo. It's not wired
up. How can it go off?

Inspector   That's true. Don't fall for it.

Maniac   All right then, Bertozzo, you know so much
about bombs. Let's see if there's one in here . . . Detonator –
look at that. Can you see? It's a longbar acoustic, I believe.

Bertozzo *slumps a little, drops the gun and the keys to the
handcuffs.*

Bertozzo   A longbar acoustic. Where did you find that?

The **Maniac** *picks up the keys and the gun.*

Maniac   In here. (*Indicating his big bag.*) I've got everything
in here. Including a tape recorder which now features all
our conversations. There we are . . .

He takes out the tape recorder and shows it to them.

Superintendent   What are you planning to do with it?

Maniac   Make a hundred copies of the tape and send it
round – to political parties, newspapers, government
ministers . . .

Superintendent   You can't. You twisted everything we
said and made us sound ridiculous.

Maniac   Does that matter really? The main thing is there'll be a thumping good scandal. So we can stand shoulder-to-shoulder in our social democracy and say, 'We are in the shit up to our necks, which is why we're walking with our heads held high.'

The lights suddenly go out.

Journalist   What's happening? Who turned out the lights?

There is a huge blast as the bomb goes off, apparently in the courtyard below.

Superintendent   Oh my God! The Maniac must have thrown the bomb out of the window. Will someone turn on the light?

Inspector   Let's keep calm. There must have been a power cut. Bertozzo, you're nearest the switch.

The lights come on. **Bertozzo** *has his hand on the switch.*

Superintendent   That's better.

Bertozzo   So what happened?

Journalist   Where's he gone?

Constable 2   Is the door locked?

Bertozzo *tries the door handle. It is locked.*

Inspector   He must have left through the window.

Everyone looks over at the window in shock and surprise.

Journalist   Oh look, I can slip my hand out of the handcuff. You see – you *can't* be too rich or thin.

Superintendent You're all right then. What about us? The madman left with the keys. Go and look out the window.

Journalist (*running over to the window*)   There's a load of people . . . He's . . . Oh, the poor thing . . . How could this have happened? Superintendent, would you like to make a statement?

A journalist again, she puts the microphone in the **Superintendent**'s *face.*

Superintendent   Well, I had just left the room, in fact . . .

Journalist   What are you talking about? You were handcuffed here.

Superintendent (*conceding*)   Yeah, all right.

Inspector   You saw – we had nothing to do with it.

Journalist   No, you didn't. I may have to rethink my position as far as the other fall is concerned.

Superintendent   Ah, exactly: the sudden darkness scared the Maniac . . .

Inspector   . . . and he threw himself like some mad animal at the only source of light – the window.

Journalist   Yes, that must be it. I'll go back to the newspaper and write this up.

Superintendent   Go, go! See you later!

Inspector   Good luck! We're here if you need us.

Constable 2   Don't be a stranger!

Bertozzo   Goodbye, love.

Journalist   Thanks! Bye!

She leaves. The policemen take keys out of their own pockets and unlock their own handcuffs. The mood is casual.

Bertozzo   Pretty girl.

The **Inspector** *gives* **Bertozzo** *a clip round the ear.*

Bertozzo   What's that for? Nothing wrong with a bit of old-world courtesy. . .

Knocking. Everyone stares at the door.

All   Come in!

The actor who played the **Maniac** *comes in, looking severe. He has a bushy black beard, a big belly and is carrying a bag.*

Bearded Man   Is this the Inspector's office, Special Branch?

All (*freeing themselves, gathering round him*)   It's you again!

Superintendent   Shouldn't he be a smashed and bleeding corpse?

Bertozzo   They're false, the beard and the beer-gut.

Inspector   This time we're really going to give you a good kicking.

All the police move in on him.

Bearded Man   For God's sake! What's the matter with you?!

Inspector   The beard's real.

Bertozzo   So's the beer-gut.

Superintendent   I'm sorry. We seem to have mixed you up with someone else. You look very similar.

Bearded Man   Is this how you receive visiting judges?!

Inspector   Judges?

Superintendent   You're a judge?

Bertozzo   What kind of judge?

Bearded Man   High Court Judge. I'm here to reopen the Inquiry into the death of the anarchist. If you don't mind, I'll start straight away . . .

The four policemen look unwell . . . Slow fade to black.

Notes

Act One, Scene One

3 *Central police headquarters, somewhere in England*: Fo
himself changed the setting of the play. In the first
version, the action of the play supposedly took place in
New York (see p. lvii). If there were, Fo added, any
resemblances with events which had recently occurred in
Italy, this was to be attributed solely to the peculiar magic
of theatre which leads to the most extravagant, zany
inventions later turning out to be pale imitations of
reality. The floor from which the anarchist fell was the
fourteenth floor in New York, but the fourth floor in
Milan. That apart, whatever pretence is adopted, Milan
1969 is where the action unfolds.

The stage directions are much more copious and detailed
in the English than in the Italian. Fo himself was
indifferent to such matters, and indeed to all that
pertained to publication. Where they were given, they
were the work of Franca Rame.

Bertozzo: the other police officers are referred to simply
by rank, but have equivalents in the original affair.
Bertozzo has some resemblances to Antonino Allegra, a
commissario.

In English, the impersonator has been labelled variously
'Madman' or, as here, 'Maniac'. He has no equivalent in
life, but has roots in the Italian theatre tradition, notably
with the figure of Harlequin.

5 *Professor Anthony Clare*: a psychiatrist, author of several
books and presenter of radio and television programmes
in which celebrities are invited to undertake a form of
self-analysis and discuss the formative events in their
lives.

Freud: Sigmund Freud, founder of psychoanalysis.
Obviously, the quotation is cheerfully bogus.

Professor Anthony Rabbi: Fo's play is carefully structured, with exchanges of sheer comic nonsense worthy of Edward Lear intertwined with other moments where the actual reports of the death of the anarchist are subjected to scrutiny. This is a passage of surreal clowning which sets the mood of knockabout farce and establishes the Maniac as a person of quick wit and unusual verbal dexterity, but where only the most uselessly pedantic of individuals will attempt to extract coherent meaning.

7   *you're saner than I am*: and of course in a sense he is, even if he had been described on the previous page as 'mental'. There are some key lines sprinkled even in the midst of this outlandish, capricious banter. In a world which is itself insane and unjust, the Maniac is, paradoxically, the representative of reason, decency, honesty and good sense. Far from indicating mental imbalance, his insanity is purely a theatrical device.

8   *ISA . . . Tessa*: savings plans in the UK.
I'd love to play a judge: Fo begins to point forward, very subtly, to the content of his play, and to the subjects which would have been in the mind of his first audience. The topic under examination involves a miscarriage of justice as well as an abuse of power.

9   *I love it here . . . I feel safe*: a further ironic glimpse forward at what happened to Pinelli in the police station, where he was anything but safe.

10   *I'll throw myself out of the window*: unobtrusively, the discussion slides towards the tragedy of Pinelli.

11   *Judge's Decision To Terminate*: there was such an inquiry carried out by Judge Giovanni Caizzi who concluded that Pinelli's death was an accident, and that no further proceedings were required.
Inspector Throws-Anarchists-Out-the-Windows: this is an obvious allusion to Luigi Calabresi, the *commissario* of police who interrogated Pinelli and who rejoiced in this nickname among the criminal fraternity of Milan. He had, it was alleged, developed the habit of inviting suspects to take a seat on the window ledge of his office from which there was a sheer drop on to the courtyard

below. He and his colleagues would then throw taunts at them, challenging them to jump.

12 *mercenary outfit in Bosnia*: in the original, Fo introduced references not to Bosnia but to a prison camp in the south of Italy to which anti-fascists were sent during the Fascist regime. The camp had been run by Marcello Guida, who was chief of police in Milan at the time of Piazza Fontana and the arrest of the anarchists, and model for the Superintendent.

13 *Huddersfield*: in Italian, Fo's Maniac threatened the Inspector with a posting to the town of Vibo-Valenzia in Calabria, which allowed him to make puns with Calabresi's name.

   To work, you old judge you: Fo commonly follows the Italian tradition of *commedia dell'arte* in inserting places for the display of *lazzi,* the devising of stage business or passages left to the inventiveness of actors, giving them the opportunity to demonstrate their performance skills, here the impersonation of a judge.

14 *male dancer*: Pietro Valpreda, the other anarchist arrested while Pinelli was still in custody, was a dancer by profession.

Act One, Scene Two

17 *nervous tic:* several observers at the hearing of the libel case Calabresi brought against Baldelli noted the compulsive, involuntary movements of the jaw and the different nervous habits Luigi Calabresi (the Inspector) had developed.

18 *that open window*: no matter how seemingly whimsical the comic situation he has set up, Fo never allows attention to stray too far from the mystery of the death of the anarchist, and the enigma of the window left open in winter in Milan.

22 *Another generation, you see, old school*: in the original Italian, this remark was more loaded than the more innocuous English. Marcello Guida (the Superintendent), the chief of police in Milan, had been commandant of an

internment camp under Fascism. Fo maintains a play on
this fact for the next couple of exchanges in the Italian.

23   *an anarchist*: Fo begins to focus on the inquiry which is
the subject matter of this play, but without altering the
tone. He maintains the seemingly flippant, off-hand,
comic repartee which is appropriate to farce.

in the early stages: once again, a remark which is more
loaded than it seems on the surface. Under pressure from
journalists and investigators, there were many stages, and
many alterations to the police version of what happened
that night.

raptus: this term, meaning a 'seizure' or an 'overwhelming
impulse', is pseudo-jargon, and no more common in
Italian than in English. Bandieu is an invention of Fo's,
created to ridicule the report prepared by Judge Amati,
who peppered his pages with references to learned
medical and legal authorities on the different motivations
and categories of suicide. Amati's conclusion was that
Pinelli was not to be numbered among those who had
long nurtured plans to take their own lives, but among
those who are moved by a sudden, unpredictable and
irresistible inner force – a raptus.

Let's re-construct: the Maniac makes the officers embark
on a play-within-a-play.

24   *on the twenty-fifth*: on 25 April 1969, there were bombs
placed at the Fiat stand in Milan Exhibition Centre,
injuring nineteen people, and at the city's railway station,
this time without casualties. Commissario Calabresi
headed the police operation, and the judge, Amati, who
conducted the second inquiry into the death of Pinelli,
was in charge of judicial proceedings. A total of eight
suspects, two anarchists, two communists and four
members of other left-wing organisations were arrested.
Two of the accused were released after seven months in
prison, and the other six were acquitted when the
prosecution case at the trial, which opened on 22 March
1971, fell apart. The defence team asked for proceedings
to be opened against Calabresi for inducing witnesses to
give false evidence.

25 *eight months ago*: at the time of the first presentation of
    the play.
    only anarchist railwayman: these are more or less
    verbatim quotes from one of the reports. Antonino
    Allegra, head of the Political Section of the Milan police
    force, asked Pinelli how many anarchist railway workers
    there were in Milan. When he replied that he was the only
    one, Allegra is said to have retorted, 'So it was you who
    placed the bombs in Central Station.'
    bombs that went off at the Law Courts: on 12 December
    1969, the day of the Piazza Fontana bombing, there were
    other explosions in Milan and Rome, three in or near
    banks, two near the 'Altar of the Fatherland' in Rome,
    which contains the tomb of the Unknown Soldier. In
    point of pedantic fact, there were no explosions at courts
    of law that day, but there were previously and
    subsequently.

26 *you'd know all about hounding*: in his previous role as
    commandant in a camp for anti-fascist activists.
    the dancer chap: Pietro Valpreda, the other suspect in the
    bombings, was arrested on 15 December. He felt that he
    was caught up in the whole business by chance, since he
    was reporting to the police station on an unrelated matter
    when he was arrested and taken to Rome. He was indeed
    a member of 22 March, a Roman anarchist circle, which,
    it later transpired, was not only infiltrated by police
    informers, but had actually been set up by one such
    informer, the fascist Mario Merlino. Valpreda was a
    dancer.

27 *alibi*: Pinelli always insisted that he had known nothing
    about the bombing, since between 4.00 and 5.30 on the
    day in question, he had been with two elderly friends in a
    bar in the Navigli, the canal district of Milan, playing
    cards. Late in the afternoon, he turned up at the anarchist
    club in the city to discover that a police raid was under
    way. He was invited by the police to accompany them to
    the police station and actually rode to the station on his
    motorbike, following the police cars. Another anarchist
    who received the same invitation fled and was later

granted political asylum in Switzerland.

'obviously the act of a guilty man': the words, 'a kind of self-accusation', were spoken by Marcello Guida in the course of an impromptu press conference held on the night of 15–16 December, shortly after Pinelli's death-plunge. In Fo's original, these words are spoken by the Superintendent.

concrete proof . . . good lad: words like these were indeed spoken by Guida and Calabresi respectively, in the weeks following the death of Pinelli.

Olympic standard in mistake-making: even if delivered in the part of, as the audience is aware, a deranged impersonator, the words spoken constitute a devastating summary of the case and an incrimination of the police. They reflect a large section of contemporary opinion. The laughter gives way to a section which is totally serious. The words of the Maniac, in the midst of a farce, are a systematic dismantling of the police case. There is a rhythm, a carefully worked series of sequences throughout this work, where serious interludes are followed by episodes of slapstick. The laughter is now stilled. Anger takes over.

longer than is legally permissible: Italian law then permitted the holding of a suspect for an initial period of forty-eight hours. In Pinelli's case, not only was the period exceeded, but he had apparently been deprived of food for three days.

28 *end of anarchy*: one of the more colourful phrases attributed to Pinelli when he was told that Valpreda had incriminated him. In Italian, the same word is used for the doctrine of 'anarchism' and the state of 'anarchy'.

29 *an old saying*: Fo is very fond of this supposed 'old saying', and quotes it a couple of times in different plays. In the original, he says explicitly that it is an English proverb. The policemen are now left to contemplate their dismal future, as the Maniac reminds them that they are no more than the necessary scapegoats, who will be abandoned by the powers that be now that the going has got rough.

33 *'Ferment a little subversion' . . . calls for a state
   clampdown!'*: this passage ends with a statement of the
   aims and objectives of the 'strategy of tension' which lay
   behind the neo-fascist campaign of terror.
   I made it all up: new departure. The Maniac now changes
   tack and adopts another persona. Having made his point
   as investigator and prosecutor, he now reverts to being
   mischief-maker, leader of the revels, instigator of impish
   nonsense.

35 *the journalist standing in the courtyard*: the journalist in
   question was Aldo Palumbo, of the communist daily,
   L'Unità. Palumbo was coming out of the press-room in
   the police station when he heard the thud of a body
   falling on the ground in the courtyard. He said that the
   fall occurred between one and four minutes after
   midnight. The problem for the police was that at that
   time an ambulance had already been called from
   Calabresi's office. The call was logged at a few minutes
   before midnight. Palumbo's timing was crucial since, if it
   was correct, it meant that the ambulance was summoned
   before the body hit the ground. His assertions gave rise to
   another theory of what happened that night in Calabresi's
   office, that the police had panicked after unintentionally
   injuring or even killing Pinelli. They then summoned an
   ambulance, but disposed of the body before it arrived.
   There were other discrepancies over the timing of the
   night's events.

36 *four cocking hours*: the Maniac cheerfully leads the police
   up and down the garden path.
   Bakunin: Mikhail Bakunin (1814–76), the Russian
   thinker who can be viewed as one of the seminal figures
   of modern anarchism. There are many strands to
   anarchism, but Bakunin, who spent several years in Italy
   in the 1860s, was the decisive figure for the development
   of anarchist thought and practice in Italy.

37 *in an unassailable position*: the onstage policemen relax,
   even if unwittingly continuing to damn themselves out of
   their own mouths and providing the audience with
   further information from the judicial inquest.

38 *a third version*: new phase. The investigation into the
history of that night is now, at least temporarily, closed.
Fo resumes the mood of zany, nonsensical, hilarious farce
as he invents a totally fictitious scene to help the officers
out.

42 *anarchist's poor widow*: Licia Pinelli did indeed phone the
police station that night after hearing reports that her
husband had thrown himself from the window. The reply
from the officer was that they had too much to do to
answer her enquiries.
your favourite anarchist protest songs: Fo himself closed
Act One with the internationalist anthem of Italian
anarchists, 'The Whole World Is Our Fatherland'. Other
directors have chosen the 'Internationale', while for the
first production of this translation the directors preferred
a hip-hop number, 'Don't Believe the Hype'.

Act Two

43 '*Our campaign of misinformation . . .*': this is not a
quote. The inverted commas have been added by the
translator.

44 *six of us*: Marcello Guida (the Superintendent) was absent
from the office, leaving the constables, Inspector
Calabresi, and another officer, Savino Lo Grano. Lo
Grano is the man who was promoted from *tenente* to
capitano. It is difficult to find exact equivalents between
ranks in the British and Italian police, but it was
remarked that involvement in this affair did not damage
the careers of the officers concerned.

46 *Monday gang*: there was such a gang, allegedly operating
in the town of Bergamo in the late sixties. The gangsters
complained, successfully, of police brutality after their
arrest.

47 *the limping anarchist dancer*: Dario Fo has frequently
complained that reality outstrips even the most creative
imagination. Pietro Valpreda suffered from a condition
which gave him a limp.
Liberty lampshades: in Italian, the term 'Liberty', taken

from the famous shop in London, is used in the sense of art nouveau. The judge, Amati, in his investigation made much of the fact that during the searches of the houses of the anarchist suspects, he found the equipment for making glass shades and for threading pearls on to Tiffany lampshades. The judge believed, or at least implied, that these implements could double as bomb-making tools.

48 *Sex and Anarchy*: the police can be forgiven for not having read this book, since there is no such work. The German Otto Weininger (1880–1903) did write several books, some of which were translated into Italian. There is an strong anti-semitic streak to his thought, and he believed that *fin de siècle* Decadentism was responsible for undermining masculinity and introducing an unhealthy cult of the feminine into mainstream culture. *pretending*: the Maniac is still in his role as mischief-maker.

49 *a single bloody word of it*: by now the dismantling of the official version is complete.

51 *A leg-up?*: the first published edition of this play (1973) was accompanied by pencil drawings by Fo showing the athleticism Pinelli would have had to display in order to dodge the police officers in a cramped space before leaping nimbly over the guard-rail of the window to accomplish his fatal jump. As La Comune wrote in their collective foreword to the first version: 'We insist in seeing the death of the anarchist not as an "out-of-the-ordinary episode" but as a "professional incident". On this point, we must keep our eyes wide open [. . .] In the light of the leap from the fourteenth floor, all that remains for us is to reconstruct a line of thought, excluding all possibility of deviation and hesitation in face of the revolutionary objective which Marxism-Leninism has taught us.'

52 *his shoe came off in my hand*: several different versions of the supposed efforts of the police officers to prevent Pinelli from jumping were produced on successive days. One of the more heroic was that one officer, Vito

Panessa, grabbed hold of his foot but only succeeded in pulling off one shoe. Regrettably, journalists in the courtyard below noted that Pinelli was wearing two shoes when his body hit the ground.

53   *always assassinating monarchs*: in the early years of the twentieth century, several members of European royal families were assassinated by anarchists, including King Umberto I of Italy in 1900.

54   *a journalist*: in the original, she was named Maria Felletti, and was based on the investigative reporter and author, Camilla Cederna, whose writings and book on the affair provided Fo with ideas and information which he incorporated into his play. This entrance marks a new beginning, with a new style. She is a political mouthpiece, who delivers direct, straight views that were previously expressed through laughter. As written by Dario Fo, her part is deadly serious, not to say dull, but to compensate and to maintain the tone of farce, the antics of the Maniac become increasingly outrageous.

55   *sexually confident and powerful looking*: and she may very well be 'sexually confident' and the rest, but it is only in English that it is considered necessary to depict her as this caricature. In Italian, she does not use the provocative banter of 'darling' etc.

57   *letter sent by a young anarchist in prison*: the letter was sent by an anarchist who was an inmate of San Vittore prison in Milan.

58   *glass eye*: the task of unravelling the activities in the station is left to the journalist, so the Maniac transmogrifies into a clown figure, with all the accompanying jollity the part requires. However, he blithely switches side as the interview continues.
     the trajectory taken by the body: this was a subject of anxious debate in the newspapers in the weeks after the death. The sketches which Fo drew for the first edition illustrate the possible angles of the fall, depending on whether or not Pinelli was still alive when his body emerged from the window. These line drawings, accompanied by precisely worded captions, illustrate the

movement which the body must have taken as it bends
expertly over the rail, hands perfectly positioned, legs
folding at the right moment to allow it to fall at a fixed
distance from the wall of the building.

59 *ambulance*: see note to p.35.

60 *a rumour*: in the frantic atmosphere of statement and
counter-statement, of rumour and pre-emptive denial, the
most fantastic stories were given credence by journalists
desperate for some new angle. This tale was reported in
various quarters. The one true fact in this tale was that a
large bruise was found on Pinelli's neck.

61 *'accidental death'*: the phrase appeared in the Public
Prosecutor Amati's report of July 1970.

62 *Oh God! My eye!*: gravity is never permitted for any
length of time. The dramatic assertions made by the
journalist are followed by a return to knockabout.
old-age pensioners: see note to p.27.

63 *capitalism in the dock*: Fo indulges in reverse irony,
playing with the expectations of his audience who, at
least at the first performances, expected to hear Fo put
capitalism in the dock.

64 *Bertozzo*: farce requires that the plot be designed and
engineered with perfect precision, so that it can move at
varying speeds. The momentum now increases, as the
characters and their roles have been fully established.
There are no more surprises for the audience. The Maniac
employs his genius for impersonation, Inspector Bertozzo
becomes increasingly frantic since he is acquainted with
the Maniac and the others behave as they must since they
are without the knowledge the two protagonists have.
The disguise adopted by the Maniac is differently
interpreted by each character, causing each to act for
reasons unknown to the others. The situation now takes
on a life of its own, justifying the knockabout, comic
violence described in the stage directions.

66 *another bomb*: the bomb planted in the Banca
Commerciale in Milan, the same day as the Piazza
Fontana bombing, failed to ignite and was discovered by
the police. Beyond all reasonable doubt, it was the work

of the same group who were behind Piazza Fontana, but instead of having it carefully rendered harmless by bomb disposal experts and examined for clues it could have provided about the manufacturers of such devices, the police exploded it that very night.

68 *Professional . . . Or military?*: this question goes to the heart of the counter-information Fo is providing in this play. The allegation contained in the question is that anarchist dilettantes could only have managed a home-made, amateurish device, while the cunningly constructed bomb was plainly the work of experts, perhaps of Italy's military. In other words, the Piazza Fontana bombing was part of a strategy – a strategy of tension – which was planned inside the upper echelons of Italian society, inside some ministry or officers' mess.

69 *local fascist*: both of these people have been named, the fascist was Mario Merlino and the police agent was one Salvatore Ippolito.

71 *the inquiry judge*: in fact this was a magistrate in Rome, who summoned Merlino and Ippolito after the bombings, and on the basis of their information was able to arrest the entire Rome anarchists' circle, the so-called 22 March, including Pietro Valpreda.

73 *industrial unrest last autumn*: the autumn of 1969, the so-called 'hot autumn', was a period of industrial unrest among trade unionists, and coincided with the beginnings of the student 'contestation'.
    big papers: in the original, the two left-wing papers in Italy, the communist daily *L'Unità* and *Lotta Continua,* the organ of the New Left.

74 *massive scandal*: scandals are, in this view, a safety valve, easily manipulated by people in power to ensure that nothing fundamental changes. The public are induced to believe that there may be one or two defects in the system, but that the status quo is fundamentally healthy, and that the blemishes can be cured inside the existing social framework. In this context, the Maniac's views are a contribution to a topic hotly debated in those days, between reform and revolution. Fo was a wholly

convinced advocate of revolution, and an opponent of mere reform. With this speech, the play widens out from the case of the dead anarchist on to the wider political panorama.

77   *bishop*: the choice of this new disguise is not arbitrary. If he never attacked Christian belief, Fo was no friend of the institutional Church, or of those who held office within it. By bringing in a bishop, he intended to include highly-placed churchmen in his satire of society, as he had done in previous plays.

80   *catharsis*: see Commentary, p. xxx. Fo wished to ensure that his plays did not produce catharsis, since he believed that this effect left spectators drained of all anger, and hence of all will to act. It has always been his conviction that laughter produced by farce is more likely to lead audiences to think over the topics discussed in the play, and would eventually lead them to action.

it only ever pretends to: plainly the list of scandals referred to in this passage changes from country to country and from year to year. In his first version, Fo included reference to the Profumo scandal in Britain in 1962. Previous English-language versions have made references to such public scandals as the affair of Anthony Blunt, the Surveyor of the Queen's Pictures who was also a Soviet spy, the Birmingham Six, the group of Irish people who were wrongly convicted of responsibility for a bomb outrage in the Midlands, and the Iran-Contra affair in the USA.

85   *heads held high*: Dario Fo changed his ending in successive rewrites of the play. The version published by Einaudi in 1974 ends with this line. The arrival from Rome of the 'real' investigative judge appointed by the Ministry to conduct the inquiry features in the first stage version of the play. The judge sits down and opens a discussion, not with the actors but directly with the audience.

Questions for Further Study

1. Is the Maniac really mad?
2. How important is the Maniac in driving the action of the play?
3. Are the policemen in *Accidental Death of an Anarchist* mere buffoons?
4. It has been said that the problem for actresses playing the journalist is that she is a serious character in a fast-moving romp. Do you agree with this judgement?
5. Is there any value in regarding *Accidental Death of an Anarchist* as a tragedy disguised as farce?
6. Do you think Dario Fo is successful in his efforts to combine farce with politics?
7. How does Dario Fo achieve his satirical aims in *Accidental Death of an Anarchist*?
8. Does *Accidental Death of an Anarchist* arouse any emotional response in the audience?
9. What is the dramatic or political point in having a second judge appear at the end of the play?
10. Dario Fo has said that his theatre is based on a mixture of 'laughter and anger'. Is this formula true in the case of *Accidental Death of an Anarchist*?
11 Are the disguises assumed by the Maniac in the second act merely symptoms of Fo's exuberant creativity, or is there some deeper point in the characters taken on by the Maniac?
12. Fo has stated that his theatre is a 'theatre of situation'. What does he mean by this comment, and what situation(s) has he created in this play?
13. What is the function of the first scene, and how closely is it linked to the central action of the play?
14. What does Dario Fo have to say about the function of 'scandal' in maintaining the political and social status quo?

15. How well-constructed is the plot of *Accidental Death of an Anarchist*?
16. Is it possible to appreciate *Accidental Death of an Anarchist* without any knowledge of the circumstances in Italy which gave rise to it?
17. Dario Fo conceived *Accidental Death of an Anarchist* as a work of 'counter-information'. What techniques does he use for this purpose?
18. Does the dominance of the Maniac and of the views he is putting forward unbalance the dramatic structure of the play?
19. 'Heavily didactic, unduly reliant on unfunny knockabout, dismal in its preachy style and clichéd distrust of police and authorities, utterly obvious in its conclusion, *Accidental Death* cannot appeal to anyone with an adult brain' (Jonathan Wild). Is there any merit in this dismissive review?
20. Fo wrote that his aim with *Accidental Death of an Anarchist* was not to help spectators free themselves of indignation, but to stoke up their anger 'so that they can take action on events'. What techniques could a director use to prevent the work seeming like dated whimsy?

Bloomsbury Methuen Drama Student Editions

Jean Anouilh *Antigone* • John Arden *Serjeant Musgrave's Dance*
Alan Ayckbourn *Confusions* • Aphra Behn *The Rover* • Edward Bond
Lear • *Saved* • Bertolt Brecht *The Caucasian Chalk Circle* • *Fear and
Misery in the Third Reich* • *The Good Person of Szechwan* • *Life of Galileo* •
Mother Courage and her Children • *The Resistible Rise of Arturo Ui* • *The
Threepenny Opera* • Anton Chekhov *The Cherry Orchard* • *The Seagull* •
Three Sisters • *Uncle Vanya* • Caryl Churchill *Serious Money* • *Top Girls*
• Shelagh Delaney *A Taste of Honey* • Euripides *Elektra* • *Medea* •
Dario Fo *Accidental Death of an Anarchist* • Michael Frayn *Copenhagen*
• John Galsworthy *Strife* • Nikolai Gogol *The Government Inspector* •
Robert Holman *Across Oka* • Henrik Ibsen *A Doll's House* • *Ghosts* •
Hedda Gabler • Charlotte Keatley *My Mother Said I Never Should* •
Bernard Kops *Dreams of Anne Frank* • Federico García Lorca *Blood
Wedding* • *Doña Rosita the Spinster* (bilingual edition) • *The House of
Bernarda Alba* • (bilingual edition) • *Yerma* (bilingual edition) • David
Mamet *Glengarry Glen Ross* • *Oleanna* • Patrick Marber *Closer* • John
Marston *Malcontent* • Martin McDonagh *The Lieutenant of Inishmore* •
Joe Orton *Loot* • Luigi Pirandello *Six Characters in Search of an Author*
• Mark Ravenhill *Shopping and F***ing* • Willy Russell *Blood Brothers*
• *Educating Rita* • Sophocles *Antigone* • *Oedipus the King* • Wole
Soyinka *Death and the King's Horseman* • Shelagh Stephenson *The
Memory of Water* • August Strindberg *Miss Julie* • J. M. Synge *The
Playboy of the Western World* • Theatre Workshop *Oh What a Lovely
War* Timberlake Wertenbaker *Our Country's Good* • Arnold Wesker
The Merchant • Oscar Wilde *The Importance of Being Earnest* •
Tennessee Williams *A Streetcar Named Desire* • *The Glass Menagerie*

Bloomsbury Methuen Drama Contemporary Dramatists

include

John Arden (two volumes)
Arden & D'Arcy
Peter Barnes (three volumes)
Sebastian Barry
Dermot Bolger
Edward Bond (eight volumes)
Howard Brenton
 (two volumes)
Richard Cameron
Jim Cartwright
Caryl Churchill (two volumes)
Sarah Daniels (two volumes)
Nick Darke
David Edgar (three volumes)
David Eldridge
Ben Elton
Dario Fo (two volumes)
Michael Frayn (three volumes)
David Greig
John Godber (four volumes)
Paul Godfrey
John Guare
Lee Hall (two volumes)
Peter Handke
Jonathan Harvey
 (two volumes)
Declan Hughes
Terry Johnson (three volumes)
Sarah Kane
Barrie Keeffe
Bernard-Marie Koltès
 (two volumes)
Franz Xaver Kroetz
David Lan
Bryony Lavery
Deborah Levy
Doug Lucie

David Mamet (four volumes)
Martin McDonagh
Duncan McLean
Anthony Minghella
 (two volumes)
Tom Murphy (six volumes)
Phyllis Nagy
Anthony Neilsen (two volumes)
Philip Osment
Gary Owen
Louise Page
Stewart Parker (two volumes)
Joe Penhall (two volumes)
Stephen Poliakoff
 (three volumes)
David Rabe (two volumes)
Mark Ravenhill (two volumes)
Christina Reid
Philip Ridley
Willy Russell
Eric-Emmanuel Schmitt
Ntozake Shange
Sam Shepard (two volumes)
Wole Soyinka (two volumes)
Simon Stephens (two volumes)
Shelagh Stephenson
David Storey (three volumes)
Sue Townsend
Judy Upton
Michel Vinaver
 (two volumes)
Arnold Wesker (two volumes)
Michael Wilcox
Roy Williams (three volumes)
Snoo Wilson (two volumes)
David Wood (two volumes)
Victoria Wood